PETER'S GIFTS

by *Frances Hesselbein*

What greater gift could there possibly be in this year of the Drucker Centennial, Peter Drucker's 100th birthday, than a *Leader to Leader* special issue for all our readers?

Not long ago, Ira Jackson, dean of the Drucker School at Claremont, and I had a bright idea. He and Rick Wartzman would find five great Drucker friends and disciples—people who knew Peter, had worked with him, understood the significance of his life and contribution—who could tell a Drucker story in a way that would illuminate Peter's gifts to leaders, organizations, societies, how he changed our lives, and how he will always be with us.

Leader to Leader Institute (formerly the Peter F. Drucker Foundation for Nonprofit Management) would do the same. Our five distinguished authors would join Claremont's five, and at the end of Peter's 100th birthday year we would celebrate with the commemorative Peter Drucker issue of *Leader to Leader.*

As honorary chairman of our Foundation, Peter wrote the lead article for the first issue of our new journal in 1993, which also carried articles by Jim Collins, John W. Gardner, Steve Kerr, and Rosabeth Moss Kanter. The title of Peter's article was "The Shape of Things to Come." Like almost everything he ever wrote, it is as relevant and as powerful today as the day he wrote it. Of all the accolades and honors Peter has received in this centennial year, I have a feeling this issue of the journal would have a very significant meaning, for all the authors had a special relationship with Peter, some for many years. They write not from theory but from the heart, from a rich, trusting personal experience.

My journey with Peter Drucker, my devotion to the Drucker philosophy, began long ago. When I took my first professional position as executive director and CEO of the Talus Rock Girl Scout Council in Johnstown, Pennsylvania, in 1970, I walked into the

...as relevant and as powerful today as the day he wrote it.

office that first morning with copies of Peter Drucker's *The Effective Executive* for each staff member. I had no idea who Peter Drucker was. I just knew his book was exactly right for our work. Six years later, when I was called to New York to become the national executive director and CEO of the Girl Scouts of the U.S.A., *The Effective Executive* traveled to New York with me, as did every book Peter had ever published and every video he ever made.

Perhaps if I share with you how I met Peter and the influence he has had upon my work, one more story could be added to the thousands of others about how Peter influenced, encouraged, and challenged leaders to be leaders. All of us treasure his wisdom, which was so generously shared.

I met Peter in 1981, when as CEO of the Girl Scouts of the U.S.A. I was invited by the chancellor of New York University to join 50 foundation and other social sector presidents for dinner, to hear the great Peter Drucker speak. I knew that in such a large group I would not have an opportunity to meet him, but I would have the opportunity to hear him live—Peter Drucker, the great thought leader who had influenced the volunteers and staff of the largest organization for girls and women in the world.

The invitation was for a 5:30 PM reception at the University Club in New York, to be followed by dinner and Professor Drucker's address. Now, if you grew up in the mountains of western Pennsylvania, 5:30 is 5:30, so I arrived promptly at the University Club, only to find myself alone with two bartenders.

I turned, and behind me was a man who had just walked in. Obviously, if one grew up in Vienna, 5:30 is 5:30. The man said, "I am Peter Drucker." Startled, I responded with, "Do you know how important you are to the Girl Scouts?" He said, "No, tell me." I replied, "If you go to any one of our 335 Girl Scout Councils, you will find a shelf of your books. If you read our corporate planning, management monographs, and study our management and structure, you will find your philosophy."

Peter said, "You are very daring. I would be afraid to do that. Tell me, does it work?"

"It works superbly well," I replied. "And I have been trying to gather up enough courage to call you and ask if I may have an hour of your time, if I may come to Claremont and lay out before you everything you say the effective organization must have in place. And I'd like to talk with you about how we can take the lead in this society and blast into the future."

Peter replied, "Why should both of us travel? I'll be in New York in several months and I'll give you a day of my time." And that was the beginning of a remarkable eight-year adventure in learning and exploration that the Girl Scouts was privileged to have with the father of modern management.

The great day came in the spring of 1981, when Peter Drucker met with members of the Girl Scouts national board and staff for the first time. He said, "You do not see yourselves as life-size. You do not appreciate the significance of the work you do, for we live in a society that pretends to care about its children, and it does not." He added, "For a little while you give a girl a chance to be a girl in a society that forces her to grow up all too soon." For the next eight years, he gave us two or three days of his time each year. He studied us, wrote about us: "Best-managed organization in the country." "Tough, hard-working women can do anything." "Frances Hesselbein could manage any company in America."

When I left the Girl Scouts of the U.S.A. on January 31, 1990 (and my last year was my most exuberant year), I bought a home in Easton, Pennsylvania,

...the power of civility...

promised a publisher I would write a book on mission, and decided that I wasn't going to travel so much. But in mid-March, six weeks later, Bob Buford, Dick Schubert, and I (all of us enormously influenced by Peter in our careers) flew to Claremont to talk about how we could spread and apply Peter's works and philosophy to the nonprofit sector. The day before Peter was to join us, we brainstormed all afternoon and evening. The result? The Peter Drucker Foundation for Nonprofit Management, a foundation that would deal not in money but in intellectual capital and that would move the Drucker philosophy across the nonprofit world.

The next morning Peter arrived to meet us, not knowing what we were up to. Newsprint covered the walls of our meeting room, and we took turns presenting our wonderful brainchild. Peter listened with no expression; we couldn't tell what he was thinking. Finally, "We will not name it for me. I am not dead yet and I do not intend to be an icon." (The only battle he ever lost.) "We will not focus on me; there are a lot of good people out there, and you will bring them in." (Already he had expanded our vision.)

Bob said that he and Dick thought I should be the chairman of the new board. After all, I had just left the Girl Scouts and would have time to chair several board meetings a year for the new Drucker Foundation. Peter's response was: "You will not be the chairman, you will be the president and CEO and run it or it won't work." So six weeks after leaving one of the largest voluntary organizations in the world, I found myself CEO of the smallest foundation in the world, with no staff and no money, just a powerful vision shared with co-founders passionate about bringing Peter Drucker to the wider world, transforming what he would soon name "the social sector" because he believed it was in this sector that we find the greatest success in meeting social needs. The rest is history, one that is well documented and alive on our Web site (www.leadertoleader.org) and in our 26 books in 28 languages that are distributed around the world. When Peter became frail, we gave back the name of the foundation to the family and took the name of our journal—becoming the Leader to Leader Institute. It is the same organization.

It is difficult to think about Peter without remembering his graciousness, the power of civility that was so much a part of who he was and how he did what he did, a gift of example. He was enormously generous with his time and his counsel. After that first transformative day, he poured his time, energy, and wisdom into the Drucker Foundation for the next twelve years. From Peter, we learned about having a passion for the vision and the mission, and thousands of our members, authors, and participants shared that passion with a new kind of exuberance as we documented his impact and influence. Above all, I had 20 unbroken years of working personally with Peter.

One great contribution was his seminal article in the July-August 1989 *Harvard Business Review,* "What Business Can Learn from Nonprofits." (Some were sure it was a typo. The article turned on its head the old view of the nonprofit sector as the junior partner of business and government.) But, Peter said, "The best-managed nonprofit is better managed than the best-managed corporation."

From 1990 on, over the next 20 years, as the Drucker Foundation and then as the Leader to Leader Institute, we captured hundreds of moments and messages that Peter gave us—his work and his messages about the nonprofit, the social sector—for he did redefine and bring new recognition and new significance to "the social sector as the equal partner of business and government." We treasure those messages still.

On our 15th anniversary, in April 2005, we celebrated Peter Drucker's life and contribution at our "Shine a Light" dinner. "Shine a Light" was appropriate that evening, and it is now, for that's what Peter did for 95 years, as he does today. His light illuminates the darkness, inspiring young people who are just discov-

Think first, speak last.

ering Peter, our young leaders of the future who are finding relevance and inspiration just as our leaders of the present have found the Drucker philosophy an indispensable companion for their journey. For the Leader to Leader Institute, it is not enough to keep his legacy alive. Instead, we will bring new energy, new resources, and new partnerships to our new challenge. Peter's light shines across the sectors, reaching leaders hungry for Peter's messages—messages that will illuminate, will change their lives, and in the end will move them to define the effective executive, the leader of the future. That will be the living legacy of Peter Drucker: vibrant, alive for a new generation, with new relevance, new challenge, new significance, and new celebration of Peter Drucker's life, his influence, his light that shines anew.

In every speech I give, in the United States and around the world—so far in 68 countries—I share Peter Drucker's legacy, his philosophy, and his messages: "Think first, speak last," and "The leader of the future asks. The leader of the past tells. Ask, don't tell." Also, "It is not business, it is not government, it is the social sector that may yet save society." I add that Peter was not a pessimist, but he was very sober about this decade.

Best of all, I love to challenge leaders everywhere to learn from Peter's observation: "I never predict. I simply look out the window and see what is visible but not yet seen."

It's all out there, the next decade that is yet to be defined. The greatest gift to Peter's memory would be for each of his followers, his fellow travelers, to "look out the window and see what is visible but not yet seen," then share that vision as our tribute to that quiet intellectual giant who changed our lives with his wisdom, courage, respect, and love.

Frances Hesselbein chairs the Board of Governors of the Leader to Leader Institute and served as its founding President. She was appointed to the Class of 1951 Chair for the Study of Leadership at The United States Military Academy at West Point in August 2009, the first woman and nongraduate of West Point to serve in this position. She was named a Senior Leader at the U.S. Military Academy at the 2008 National Conference on Ethics in America. In 1998, she was awarded the Presidential Medal of Freedom, the highest U.S. civilian honor. The award recognized her leadership as chief executive officer of the Girl Scouts of the U.S.A. from 1976 to 1990, her role as the founding president of what was then called the Drucker Foundation, and her service as "a pioneer for women, volunteerism, diversity, and inclusion."

TOWARD A NEW DRUCKER CENTURY

by Ira A. Jackson

I have the privilege—and the challenge—of serving as dean of the school named for Peter Drucker. It is the school where he taught for 35 years, where his papers are housed, and where his legacy is preserved. It's a huge privilege, because like all of Peter's disciples, I am walking in the footsteps of a pioneer—the father of management—and standing on the shoulders of an intellectual and philosophical giant. To say that mine is a humbling role would be to vastly understate the degree to which I feel like an inadequate apprentice.

The challenge of being dean of Peter's school includes the need to sustain and revitalize a great institution—The Peter F. Drucker and Masatoshi Ito Graduate School of Management, the only business school in the world named for both a thinker and a doer. Through his 39 books, countless articles, and thousands of lectures, Peter Drucker was a powerful, seminal thought leader. Masatoshi Ito, the founder and builder behind one of the world's largest retail enterprises (Japan's Ito-Yokado Group), was a successful entrepreneur who put Peter's principles into practice. The pairing of a thinker with a doer symbolizes the role we try to play in management education—approaching management as a liberal art, combining theory with practice in a way that makes a difference. Peter said that the obligation of any enterprise is to continuously innovate and market, and that progress is achieved through both continuity and change. We continue to try to preserve the best of what we've always done—deliver a values-based MBA and EMBA curriculum that explicitly challenges our students to pursue lives not only of professional success but of personal and societal significance. At the same time, we launch innovative programs, such as the first executive master's degree in arts management and the only master's degree offered jointly by a school of mathematics and a school of management.

We are especially proud of our new gateway course, which every student is required to take and which is taught by all of us on the core faculty. Called "The Drucker Difference," it provides the integrative framework for everything that follows. (McGraw-Hill will be publishing a book with that title this fall, capturing the essence of the course.) We are also thrilled with the progress of our new Drucker Institute, started less than three years ago. It has transformed the old Drucker Archives into a living memorial and a think-tank/action-tank that is bringing Peter's principles and practices to new audiences in new ways, including through the 25 Drucker Societies that have been formed from Dallas to Philadelphia, China to Mumbai, Korea to Israel, and Japan to Brazil. The Drucker Institute is becoming the hub of a growing global movement for effective management, ethical leadership, and social responsibility. Now, with the Drucker Centennial well under way, events around the world are celebrating Peter's

Effective management, ethical leadership, social responsibility...

legacy and reaffirming the relevance of his penetrating insights and prescriptions for society.

While our task is humbling, I sense that Peter would be smiling at the energy, creativity, and sense of urgency and importance behind the efforts of so many good people working to preserve and rekindle his legacy. This special issue of *Leader to Leader* is the result of a collaboration of my dear friend Frances Hesselbein and the Drucker School and Drucker Institute in Claremont. I know that it would please Peter.

Beyond institutional stewardship, the challenge extends to the need to sustain, replenish, and recapitalize Drucker's intellectual legacy. There are some 12,000 schools of business around the world, with tens of thousands of faculty and hundreds of thousands of students. Yet, as recent events so graphically remind us, the performance, effectiveness, and integrity of many organizations and their leaders around the world are lacking, deteriorating, and even collapsing. The intellectual contributions of the academy in steering us away from disaster or providing a higher standard for performance or even predicting the consequences of activities like unscrupulous subprime lending have been thin at best, and few and far between. Some have even accused the academy of contributory negligence, which may not be entirely unfair. Where, one might legitimately ask, are the contemporary Peter Druckers, with the courage and conviction to call things as they see them, who rail against the excesses, and who argue, as he did, for ethical balance, historical perspective, and personal and institutional responsibility? Too bad so many failed to take Peter's advice and pledge, as doctors have done since first taking the Hippocratic Oath, to "Above all, first and foremost, do no harm."

Peter warned that a responsible society is the only sure antidote and answer to tyranny and anarchy. He viewed the 20th century as a wasted century. We are now given another chance to do it better—by making our time the Drucker Century. For those of us in the academy, and for those who write and teach and research about leadership, Peter's profound wisdom, intellectual courage, and personal integrity stand as a constant reminder. Our task is not just to remember Peter Drucker but to ask the tough questions about the big issues facing organizations, leaders, and society as a whole. We are called by his example to think, as he did, not only as leadership scholars and management experts, but as social ecologists, concerned about the health of society—and about how to harness ethical leadership, effective management, and social responsibility to make the world a better, more sustainable place, with greater justice, beauty, and opportunity than ever before. What a noble calling—Peter summons us to set and achieve these admirable goals as we commemorate the 100th anniversary of the birth of this remarkable man.

Ira A. Jackson is the Henry Y. Hwang Dean of The Peter F. Drucker and Masatoshi Ito Graduate School of Management at Claremont Graduate University. He previously served as associate dean of the John F. Kennedy School of Government at Harvard, director of its Center for Business and Government, Massachusetts commissioner of revenue, president of the Arizona State University Foundation, and executive vice president of BankBoston.

NOW, MORE
THAN EVER

by Rick Wartzman

When a team from the Drucker Institute and our sister institution, The Peter F. Drucker and Masatoshi Ito Graduate School of Management, began considering possible slogans to mark Peter Drucker's 100th birthday, one quickly rose above the others: "Now, more than ever."

To the uninitiated, this may well seem a bit strange. After all, how can this be the watchword for an author whose first major work, *The End of Economic Man,* was published in 1939? What could possibly be topical and timely about the teachings of a man who chronicled the Great Depression and then passed away several years before the start of our own Great Recession? What could we, in this age of blogs and tweets, learn from a writer who pounded out the last of his 39 books on a bulky Brother typewriter?

Well, the short answer is an awful lot.

Consider, for instance, Drucker's warning about financial bubbles, issued during an earlier market shakeout in the late 1980s. "The average duration of a soap bubble is known," he remarked. "It's about 26 seconds. Then the surface tension becomes too great and it begins to burst. For speculative crazes, it's about 18 months."

Plenty of industry insiders have dressed up the latest financial crisis with all kinds of fancy terminology—credit-default swaps, collateralized debt obligations, naked shorts. But in Drucker's eyes, it was simple: "No matter how clever the gambler," he declared, "the laws of probability guarantee that he will lose all that he has gained, and then a good deal more."

Drucker wrote these words in the 1990s, as a different group of once-prominent enterprises—Barings, Bankers Trust, Yamaichi Securities—were destroyed by their recklessness. Now, only the names have changed: Lehman Bros., Merrill Lynch, Countrywide Financial. "In every single one of these 'scandals,'" Drucker noted a decade ago, "top management seems to have carefully looked the other way as long as trading produced profits (or at least pretended to produce them). Until the losses had become so big that they could no longer be hidden, the gambling trader was a hero and showered with money."

Drucker didn't just grumble about the dark side of business, however. More than anything, he called for a kind of healthy balance—between short-term needs and long-term sustain-

> *Every organization must assume full responsibility for its impact on whatever it touches.*

ability; between profitability and other obligations; between the specific mission of individual organizations and the common good. "Economic performance is not the only responsibility of a business," Drucker wrote. "Every organization must assume full responsibility for its impact on employees, the environment, customers, and whomever and whatever it touches."

This, of course, is exactly the type of advice that many now see as a balm for our turbulent times. Indeed, President Obama's call for "a new era of responsibility" strongly echoes Drucker's philosophy.

It is with all this in mind that we at the Drucker Institute have tailored our programming to be relentlessly focused on what matters most today—and what will matter most tomorrow. There are those who assume that our aim is to light a candle to Peter Drucker. Nothing, though, could be further from the truth. Drucker himself was a keen student of history. But he always wanted to help people create a better future, not get stuck in the past. The only way to properly honor him is to keep looking toward the horizon ourselves.

And so it is that every other week the Institute distributes *Drucker Apps,* a downloadable collection of useful insights on work and life that ties Drucker's timeless wisdom to the hottest topics of today, all delivered via the latest in 21st-century technology. Although Drucker's writing is the focal point of *Apps,* original

audio and video interviews with leading management scholars and executives are part of the package. Recent issues of *Apps* have covered bloated executive pay, the auto industry's woes, our troubled health care system, America's surge in volunteerism, the need for innovation, and other pressing issues.

Similarly, the online column that I have the privilege of writing for *Business Week,* "The Drucker Difference," links Drucker's expansive oeuvre to the latest headlines.

Other Institute programs are also squarely fixed on the here and now. Earlier this year, the Institute's managing director, Zach First, and I traveled to Amman, Jordan, to put on a seminar for a group of nearly 200 Middle Eastern executives and government officials. The central theme: What would Drucker say about the financial crisis? Drucker's brilliance will be on display, once again, this fall at the World Business Forum in New York. This symposium—featuring Bill Clinton, Jack Welch, T. Boone Pickens, Gary Hamel, and a host of other luminaries—has been officially designated a Drucker Centennial event.

Meanwhile, visiting fellows at the Drucker Institute, including British social philosopher Charles Handy and former eBay Marketplace president Rajiv Dutta, are daring to tackle some of the biggest questions of our day, just as Drucker once did. Among them: How can we balance profit and social responsibility?

Joe Maciariello, the Institute's academic director, is busy with his own cutting-edge research. His latest project aims to bring Drucker's notion of "management as a liberal art" into the nation's colleges and universities. The goal is to have business professors integrate the humanities more fully into their classes—giving their students a stronger moral compass—while liberal arts majors learn something about application and results. The intention is for these principles to ultimately transcend the academy and make their way into the realm of practice.

The Institute's newest product, "Drucker Unpacked," provides another opportunity for us to showcase how relevant Drucker's thinking remains. This engaging, do-it-yourself workshop-in-a-box distills decades of Drucker's most essential concepts so that up to 15 people in any organization can turn them into action.

Perhaps nowhere, though, can the Institute's forward-looking orientation be seen more clearly than in our burgeoning network of Drucker Societies. These all-volunteer groups—now two dozen strong in 15 countries—draw on Drucker's vast body of work for information and inspiration as they seek to effect positive change in their local communities.

By implementing a slate of programs developed in conjunction with the Drucker Institute, the Drucker Society Global Network has become a living, breathing embodiment of Peter Drucker's ideas and ideals. The Global Network's activities include book clubs in which members discuss Drucker's teachings and how to apply them to their companies and communities, Drucker-based training programs for nonprofit organizations, presentations on Drucker and his principles for high school students, and workshops on innovation for would-be entrepreneurs.

Toward the end of his life, Drucker told an interviewer, "I consider it quite likely that, three years after my death, my name will be of absolutely no advantage." It was one of the few times he was 100 percent wrong.

Four years have elapsed since Drucker died, and "Now, more than ever" isn't merely a motto. Thanks to the seminal nature of Drucker's work, the remarkable breadth and depth of his writing, his prescience, and the thousands of people around the world who are actively embracing his beliefs, Drucker's legacy is more than alive and well. It is growing stronger by the day.

Rick Wartzman is executive director of the Drucker Institute. He is a former writer and editor with The Wall Street Journal and a former business editor of the Los Angeles Times.

PETER DRUCKER'S LEGACY

by Jim Collins

Business and social entrepreneur Bob Buford once observed that Peter Drucker contributed as much to the triumph of free society as any other individual. I agree. For free society to function we must have high-performing, self-governed institutions in every sector, not just in business but equally in the social sectors. Without that, the only workable alternative is totalitarian tyranny. Strong institutions, in turn, depend directly on excellent management, and it was Drucker who virtually invented and advanced the concept of effective management as the central function in free society.

Louis Armstrong. Frank Lloyd Wright. Pablo Picasso. With each of these creators we have a "before" period and everything "after." Jazz would never be the same after Armstrong. Architecture reeled under the creative onslaught of Wright. The history of painting in the 20th century pivots around Picasso. So, too, we cannot imagine the field of management thinking without Drucker.

My first encounter with Drucker's legacy came in a discussion in graduate school, when a professor challenged my first-year class: managers and leaders—are they different? The conversation unfolded something like this:

"Leaders set the vision; managers just figure out how to get there," said one student.

"Leaders inspire and motivate, whereas managers keep things organized," said another.

"Leaders elevate people to the highest values. Managers manage the details."

The discussion revealed an underlying worship of "leadership" and a disdain for "management." Leaders are inspired. Leaders are large. Leaders are the kids with black leather jackets, sunglasses, and sheer unadulterated cool. Managers, well, they're the somewhat nerdy kids, decidedly less interesting, lacking charisma. And of course, we all wanted to be *leaders,* leaving the drudgery of management to others.

We could not have been more misguided and juvenile in our thinking. We were then introduced to Drucker's insight: *the very best leaders are first and foremost effective managers.* Leadership is, of course, vital. But those who lead without discipline—those who fail to manage—will become either irrelevant or dangerous, not only to their organizations but to society. The shattered economy of 2008–2009, populated by once-great enterprises that authored their own demise, drives home the point. I believe that Drucker's teachings, properly applied, would have helped many aggressively led enterprises stay on a more sustainable course. We need Drucker's writings as much as ever, and we ignore Drucker's fundamental teachings at our peril.

My second encounter with Drucker's impact came at Stanford in the early 1990s, when Jerry Porras and I were researching the great corporations of the 20th century. The more we dug into the formative stages and inflection points of companies like General Electric, Johnson & Johnson, Procter & Gamble, Hewlett-Packard, Merck, and Motorola, the more we saw Drucker's intellectual fingerprints. David Packard's notes and speeches from the formative years of HP so mirrored Drucker's writings that I conjured up an image of Packard giving management sermons with a classic Drucker text in hand. When we finished our research, Jerry and I struggled to name our book, rejecting more than 100 titles. Finally in frustration I blurted, "Why don't we just name it *Drucker Was Right,* and we're done!" (We later named the book *Built to Last.*)

What accounts for Drucker's enormous impact? I believe the answer lies not just in his specific ideas, but in his entire *approach* to ideas, one composed of four elements:

- He looked out the window, not in the mirror.

- He started first—and always—with results.

- He asked audacious questions.

- He infused all his work with a concern and compassion for the individual.

I once had a conversation with a faculty colleague about the thinkers who had influenced us. I mentioned Drucker. My colleague wrinkled his nose, and said: "Drucker? But he's so *practical.*" Drucker would have loved that moment of disdain, reveling in being criticized for the fact that his ideas worked. They worked because he derived them by precise observation of empirical facts. He pushed always to look *out there,* in the world, to derive ideas, challenging himself and his students with "Look out the

The best leaders are first and foremost effective managers.

window, not in the mirror!" Drucker falls in line with thinkers like Darwin, Freud, and Taylor—empiricists all. Darwin filled notebooks with his observations about pigeons and turtles. Freud used his therapeutic practice as a laboratory. Taylor conducted experiments, systematically tracking thousands of details. Like them, Drucker immersed himself in empirical facts and then asked, "What underlying principle explains these facts, and how can we harness that principle?"

Drucker belonged to the church of results. Instead of starting with an almost religious belief in a particular set of answers—a belief in leadership, or culture, or information, or innovation, or decentralization, or marketing, or strategy, or any other category—Drucker began first with the question "What accounts for superior results?" and *then* derived answers. He started with the outputs—the definitions and markers of success—and worked to discover the inputs, not the other way around. And then he preached the religion of results to his students and clients, not just to business corporations but equally to government and the social sectors. The more noble your mission, the more he demanded: What will define superior performance? "Good intentions," he would seemingly yell without ever raising his voice, "are no excuse for incompetence."

And yet while practical and empirical, Drucker never became technical or trivial. Nor did he succumb to the trend in modern academia to answer (in the words of the late John Gardner) "questions of increasing irrelevance with increasing precision." By remaining a professor of management and seeing management

"Drucker? But he's so practical."

not as a science but as a liberal art—he gave himself the freedom to pursue audacious questions. Drucker passionately believed in management—not as a technocratic exercise but as a profession with a noble calling, just like the very best of medicine and law. One of my early encounters with Drucker's writings came on a vacation in Monterey, California. My wife and I embarked on one of our adventure walks through a bookstore, treasure hunting for unexpected gems among the used books. I came across a beaten-up, dog-eared copy of his 1946 book, *Concept of the Corporation,* expecting a tutorial on how to build a company. But after a few pages, I realized that it asked a much bigger question: What is the proper role of the corporation at this stage of civilization? Drucker had been invited to observe General Motors from the inside, and the more he saw, the more disturbed he became. "General Motors . . . can be seen as the triumph and the failure of the technocrat manager," he later wrote. "In terms of sales and profits [GM] has succeeded admirably. . . . But it has also failed abysmally—in terms of public reputation, of public esteem, of acceptance by the public." He wrote these words when GM still sat as one of the most powerful enterprises in the world, when the idea of putting "General Motors" and "failure" in the same sentence would have seemed more delusional than prophetic. But now, as I write these words in 2009, GM has been taken over by the federal government in a desperate move to stave off utter collapse. Drucker would likely not have been pleased to see the culmination of this arc of tragedy, but I suspect he would have used it as a fascinating, if perverse, marker of the evolving relationship between business corporations and society.

Drucker could be acerbic and impatient, a curmudgeon. But beneath the prickly surface, and behind every page in his works, stands a man with tremendous compassion for the individual. He sought not just to make our economy more productive but to make all of society more productive *and* more humane. To view other human beings as merely a means to an end, rather than as ends themselves, struck Drucker as profoundly immoral. And as much as he wrote about institutions and society, I believe that he cared most deeply about the individual.

I personally experienced Drucker's concern and compassion in 1994, when I found myself at a crossroads, trying to decide whether to jettison a traditional path in favor of carving my own. I mentioned to an editor of *Industry Week* that I admired Peter Drucker. "I recently interviewed Peter," he said, "and I'd be happy to ask if he'd be willing to spend some time with you."

I never expected anything to come of it, but one day I got a message on my answering machine. "This is Peter Drucker"—slow, deliberate, in an Austrian accent—"I would be very pleased to spend a day with you, Mr. Collins. Please give me a call." We set a date for December, and I flew to Claremont, California. Drucker welcomed me into his home, enveloping my extended hand into two of his. "Mr. Collins, so very pleased to meet you. Please come inside." He invested the better part of a day sitting in his favorite wicker chair, asking questions, teaching, guiding and challenging. I made a pilgrimage to Claremont seeking wisdom from the greatest management thinker, and I came away feeling that I'd met a compassionate and generous human being who—almost as a side benefit—was a prolific genius.

At the end of our long conversation, he admonished me to worry less about survival and success, and to worry more about how to be *useful.* His comment stung, like being whapped by a metaphorical bamboo stick from a Zen master, snapping me back to the central lessons in *The Effective Executive.* In that short, readable book, Drucker set forth the principles of individual effectiveness long before such treatises became fashionable, and set forth his passionate conviction that such effectiveness lies not in genetic traits but in learnable disciplines. Manage your time, not your work. Know your priorities: do first

Worry less about success, more about how to be useful.

things first, and do not multi-task. Results come primarily from building on strength, not shoring up weakness. But above all, replace the quest for success with the quest for contribution. The critical question is not, "How can you achieve?" but "What can you contribute?"

Drucker's own contribution was not a single idea but an entire body of work that has one gigantic advantage: nearly all of it is essentially right. Drucker had an uncanny ability to develop insights about the workings of the social world, and to later be proved right by history. His first book, *The End of Economic Man,* published in 1939, sought to explain the origins of totalitarianism; after the fall of France in 1940, Winston Churchill made it a required part of the book kit issued to every graduate of the British Officers' Candidate School. His *Concept of the Corporation* so rattled senior management by its accurate foreshadowing of future challenges to the corporate state that it was essentially banned at GM during the Sloan era. Drucker's 1964 book was so far ahead of its time in laying out the principles of corporate strategy that his publisher convinced him to abandon the title *Business Strategies* in favor of *Managing for Results,* because the term "strategy" was utterly foreign to the language of business. His seminal work, *Management,* first published more than three decades ago and recently revised by his Claremont colleague Joseph Maciariello, still stands as *the* definitive text on the principles of management.

There are two ways to change the world: the pen (the use of ideas) and the sword (the use of power). Drucker chose the pen, and thereby rewired the brains of thousands who carry the sword. Those who choose the pen have an advantage over those who wield the sword: the written word never dies. If you never had the privilege of meeting Peter Drucker, you can get to know him

through his writings. You can converse with him. You can write notes to him in the margins. You can argue with him, be irritated by him, and become inspired by him. He can mentor you, if you let him, teach you, challenge you, change you—and through you, the world you touch.

Peter Drucker shone a light in a dark and chaotic world, and his words remain as relevant today as when he banged them out on his cranky typewriter decades ago. They deserve to be read by every person of responsibility, now, tomorrow, 10 years from now, 50, and 100. That free society triumphed in the 20th century guarantees nothing about its triumph in the 21st; centralized tyranny remains a potent rival, and the weight of history is not on our side. When young people ask, "What can I do to make a difference?" they would do well to follow some Druckerian advice: Get your hands on an organization aligned with your passion, if not in business, then in the social sector. If you can't find one, start one. And then lead it—through the practice of management—to deliver extraordinary results and to make such a distinctive impact that you multiply your own impact a thousandfold.

Jim Collins is coauthor of "Built to Last" and author of "Good to Great," "Good to Great and the Social Sectors," and "How the Mighty Fall." This essay is adapted from his forewords to "Management" (revised edition) and "The Daily Drucker."

THE LAST TIME
I SAW PETER
DRUCKER

by Marshall Goldsmith

Peter Drucker was always a hero to me.

More than 20 years ago I was introduced to Peter by my great friend Frances Hesselbein. Since then I have served on the board of the Peter Drucker Foundation (now the Leader to Leader Institute). I had the privilege of spending more than 50 full days with Peter, and enjoying many lunches and dinners with him. I will forever be grateful to Frances for many reasons; one is for having given me the opportunity to meet Peter Drucker and learn so much from just being around him.

In 2005, I got a message from Frances that Peter was probably going to die soon, and, if I wanted to see him, now would be the time. This was a very hard decision for me. I tried to put myself in his shoes. I asked myself, "If I were near death, would I want a man who admired me (and was 40 years younger than me) seeing me in a declining state, or would I want this person to remember me as I was?"

I contemplated this question for several hours, and then decided that there is no way to really understand what it is like to face death until you are there. I not only couldn't answer the question from Peter's perspective, I couldn't even answer it for myself.

Finally, I decided to go to Claremont and visit Peter at his home. As is normal for me, I had been on the road and did not have my own car. Rather than take a taxi from the airport, I decided to use a car service, so I could leave the car outside and be ready to leave instantly if my visit seemed awkward or embarrassing.

My reasons for wanting to visit Peter had as much to do with my own needs as with my concern for his needs. I wanted to have a final chance to thank Peter Drucker for everything he had done to help me have a better life. My first book was called *The Leader of the Future.* My coeditors were Frances Hesselbein and Richard Beckhard. The book was published by Jossey-Bass and the Drucker Foundation, and Peter wrote the foreword. To say that I was the junior member of a team involving Hesselbein, Beckhard, and Drucker would be an understatement. I felt honored to even be mentioned in the company of such great people.

Over the years, Peter always had time to ask about my wife, family, life, and career, to answer my questions and help me however he could. He not only helped me, he was kind enough to

Peter was always a realist.

give great counsel to my children. I wanted to say thank-you before it was too late.

For some reason, I am almost never nervous. I have frequently spoken in front of thousands of people and not been bothered at all. But as the car approached Peter's home for our last visit, I began to feel nervous. I was very worried. I wanted to do what was right but couldn't quite figure out what that meant.

When I entered his home, I instantly felt at ease. I talked with Doris, Peter's wife, for a couple of minutes. Then she left us alone to talk to each other. I ended up staying for 45 minutes. We had a wonderful conversation.

Peter was always a realist. He knew that he was going to die and why I was there. To go through the pretense of "I am sure everything is going to be fine," or "You really look great" would have been an insult to him. We just started talking about life.

After I was able to thank Peter for all that he had done to help me, we talked about many topics related to economics, management, and the history of the world. As always, he was amazing!

One of the reasons that Peter Drucker was such a great man is that he had a wonderful sense of history. He was brought up in an environment where people spent hours discussing history, philosophy, and world events. As a young man he listened to a wide range of psychologists, sociologists, economists, philosophers, and historians. He developed a wide and rich knowledge base, one that gave him a unique perspective on life. He spent so many years studying the grand drama of human existence that he was able to see well beyond the fads and programs of the year that excite so many people in the field of management. Peter Drucker excelled at describing the future because he had a deep understanding of the past. In hindsight, many of Peter's writings were astonishing! To give only a few examples, he predicted, with uncanny accuracy, the rise of Japan as an economic power, the fall of the Soviet empire,

the emergence of the information society, and the increasing impact of the knowledge worker.

As Peter and I discussed the rise and fall of great companies, I brought up General Motors. I am far from an expert in finance, but I do have an undergraduate degree in mathematical economics. I said to Peter, "I have been 'running the numbers' and I believe that General Motors will eventually have to face bankruptcy. I cannot see any other alternative. For years, GM's management has been making promises to employees about pension and health care benefits, without having the cash to back up these promises. Their expenses are going to kill them. To make it worse, companies in India and China are eventually going to produce cars at such low cost that their *total* cost per car will be less than GM's employee benefit costs. There is no way that GM, as it exists today, can continue to compete over the next decade."

Although I greatly admired Peter Drucker, he, like most of us, had his quirks. One of his quirks was "Doesn't bear fools gladly." Peter had infinite patience for people who were serious about what they were saying and had done their homework. He was in no way an intellectual snob. On the other hand, he showed almost no patience for people who were just talking off the top of their heads and had not bothered to study seriously or think before they spoke. Before discussing GM with Peter, I thought I had done my homework and felt like I had a good idea about what I was saying.

Peter looked over his glasses at me and replied, "Marshall, you *may* be correct in your assessment. General Motors *may* well go bankrupt. On the other hand, something unique may occur. The United States government may become involved. When bankruptcy (or something like bankruptcy) for GM comes, and I agree with you that this will happen within a decade, we may well be in a recession. Our political leaders may not want to face the costs of potentially losing thousands of jobs. Michigan is a large state that can influence presidential elections."

He went on to describe a potential future in a way that was so accurate that it now seems eerie. "I definitely believe the government will become involved," he continued. "Our political leaders will debate the merits of a normal bankruptcy versus a quasi bankruptcy that has similar results, but they will decide to will a different approach. Normal

There is a huge difference between intelligence and wisdom.

bankruptcies take too much time. Our political leaders will not want to put our country and our economy through that much uncertainty. Too many GM suppliers would be lost in a lengthy court process. Whatever happens will have to be different than the norm and it will have to be fast."

Peter Drucker's ability to visualize the future was almost frightening in its accuracy.

Looking back, I see that my final conversation had an outcome that I would never have predicted. I was concerned that I would see a person whose mental health was failing. Instead, our last meeting left me with memories of a person whose brilliance still shone in spite of his failing health, a person whose insights were so deep that they would all become validated—five years later.

In hindsight, I am not embarrassed by my level of insight. I was able to predict that General Motors would file for bankruptcy years before it happened. While this may seem obvious now, it was definitely not obvious at the time. In fact, GM stock went *up* over 75 percent between Peter's death and its peak price. If impending bankruptcy were so obvious, why did so many analysts recommend buying GM stock, and why did so many investors lose billions of dollars betting that it would succeed?

Compared to Peter Drucker's, my level of insight was like a child's. He not only predicted the problem, he predicted the ramifications of the problem, how it would impact our society, and how our government would have to deal with it!

Compared to the wisdom of Peter Drucker, many of today's so-called experts also seem like children. Our current economic crisis was partly caused by 29-year-old math

Ph.D.'s whose investment models and projections were based on their understanding of a "history" that only went back a few decades. There is a huge difference between intelligence and wisdom. Those faulty models of the future were developed by people who had plenty of intelligence but very little wisdom.

Peter Drucker had intelligence and wisdom. He was a great person. He will always be missed by me and missed by the world.

Although he is no longer with us physically, his wonderful spirit and profound ideas remain.

I have had the privilege of giving talks or writing books and articles that have been heard or read by millions of people. If I can impart even a small amount of Peter Drucker's wisdom to the people I reach, I will feel just fine about my contribution to the world.

If, when I am dying, one person feels about me the way I felt about Peter Drucker, I will be proud.

Marshall Goldsmith is the million-selling author of The Wall Street Journal *best sellers "Succession: Are You Ready" and "What Got You Here Won't Get You There"—the Harold Longman Award winner for Best Business Book of the Year. He has been recognized as one of the world's leading executive educators and coaches in almost every major business publication. His writings and videos are available online at www.MarshallGoldsmithLibrary.com.*

PETER DRUCKER AS A MENTOR AND FRIEND

by Bob Buford

P eter Drucker changed my life—utterly. I have a lot of relationships, but I can say with perfect candor that, with the exception of the love affair I have with my beautiful wife of 48 years, Linda, the 23-year working partnership I had with Peter meant the most to me. Its impact has been and still is incalculable.

My First In-Person Meeting with Peter Drucker

For me, going to meet Peter Drucker was at first something like Dorothy and the Tin Man approaching the green castle of the Wizard of Oz—except that Peter was the real thing, not a little man behind a curtain, and more real than I could have imagined. Expecting I knew not what, I walked from Griswold's, a fraying and in-need-of-much-repair-that-never-came-to-pass faux-California-Spanish low-rise hotel, four blocks to Peter's home. The weather was California balmy, but I was fully suited up for this occasion in my best fall-weight herringbone wool suit, a paisley tie pulled carefully and not too comfortably into place. I was 42 years old.

The full weight of managing a family business had descended on my shoulders ten years earlier, at age 32. My mother, the pioneering founder of a television broadcasting company, had met her death in a hotel fire at the Fairmont in Dallas—as it turned out, the result of a chafing dish igniting overnight. I was told of her death by a deputy sheriff who turned up at my front door.

I was the oldest of three sons and from that time on I was the oldest family member. I was determined to become wealthy in the broadcasting business, where the rising tide of America's insatiable appetite for television was lifting all boats, mine included.

My objective, starting from a small base, was to outgrow, in terms of percentage, all the public companies in this business. That's pretty much what happened. Beginning in 1971, the year of my pioneer mother's death—which followed one happy and two disastrous marriages—the company's market value grew at more than 25 percent a year for a dozen years, very heady times. I read not long ago that only 1 percent of companies grow at more than 15 percent a year for 10 consecutive years. I was very determined and very fortunate.

But that's getting ahead of the story. Walking that morning in the clear air (clearer then than now), I could see why people were moving to California. The weather was motion-picture-caliber beautiful. The yards were landscaped way beyond what the Texas heat would tolerate. There was a sense of pride in those lawns and gardens. I was eager and filled with anticipation.

My admiration for Peter Drucker was based entirely on his ideas. As a young and naive manager, I had read everything I could get my hands on. Much of it seemed either trendy—designed more to sell books than to guide behavior. (Remember Robert Townsend of Avis fame?) There was also an abundance of superficial pop psychobabble for hire on bookshelves and through seminars at the local Holiday Inn. Faddish. Here today, gone tomorrow. It was kind of like eating cotton candy at the state fair before the Texas-OU game, an important ritual for me each October. The game had mythic status and long-remembered significance—the cotton candy evaporated in my mouth—sticky sweet for a moment and quickly gone.

Peter Drucker was something different—whole orders of magnitude different. Deeply rooted in astonishing social observation, Peter towered above all the rest. I had continued accumulating but long since quit reading articles in the *Harvard Business Review*—that is, all those except for Peter Drucker's. One wag spoke of *HBR* as "People who can't write writing for people who don't read."

Following Peter's wisdom was analogous to investing in an index fund. He wasn't always right, but he beat the market 80 percent of the time.

Peter's thinking, so highly principled, felt as solid as granite to me. Peter wrote from a perspective that gave me the steel girders that framed the business practices that guided me through a forest of here-today-gone-tomorrow concepts. Peter had authority. Peter had gravitas. Peter brought insight, perspective, and context, where others spoke of mechanics and calculation.

Beyond that, Peter's ideas for navigating the *human* side of enterprise resonated deeply. I was moral, but not moralistic. I founded my business on ideas, but I was not ideological. In Peter, I found a soul mate.

Peter towered above all the rest.

At last I understood the principles that were fundamental to understanding human interaction—not just the headline stuff but the assumptions that were at the heart of things across centuries. They became my Golden Rules. As Jim Collins later said in the foreword to *The Daily Drucker*:

"Drucker's primary contribution is not a single idea, but rather an entire body of work that has one gigantic advantage: nearly all of it is essentially right. Drucker has an uncanny ability to develop insights about the workings of the social world, and to later be proved right by history."

That's *exactly* what had happened to me. For the past ten years, I had relentlessly sought out everything Peter had to say. I had said, "Yes sir, that's it." And I had been proved right.

So you can just imagine how I felt that morning. Peter's presence through his writing had been almost godlike. (He later warned me about this sort of adulation in no uncertain terms!) His authoritative voice rang like scripture for me. By that, I mean there was something liberating about pushing off from my two great sources: I chose to trust the Bible for my spiritual reference and to trust Peter for my organizational reference. I therefore didn't fret about the moral and practical rightness of these two dependable references. I could focus on execution rather than always looking over my shoulder to wonder about principles and concepts. I could focus on getting results and superior performance by operating on the platform and within the boundaries of these two sources—the spiritual and transcendent, and the practical and contemporary. And what was amazing to me was that I never found the two sources to be out of sync with one another!

I had heard Peter speak in public seminars before. I always imagined that, if I had been Moses on sacred ground enchanted by a burning bush and listening to a thundering oracle from above, the voice would have a deep, resonant tone with a European accent—just like Peter's. In the few appearances that I had experienced Peter (that's the right word for it) beforehand, and in all the appearances I have participated in afterward, he seemed to weave a magical spell. People would sit in rapt attention, transfixed by the sheer gestalt of this man. You could hear a pin drop. People were almost afraid to breathe. And it was substance, not theatrics.

At last, I was about to meet this great presence in my life in person. I was excited and full of anticipation, colored by not a little bit of intimidation. It seemed almost too good to be true. Here was the one person on earth whose opinions had the greatest impact on my life. I had carefully written eight drafts of a letter asking for a consulting day. I suppose I didn't really expect to get a positive response. After all, I was the CEO of a small, private (*very* private) family company that nobody knew anything about. I was young, while here was a man sought out by General Motors and Jack Welch. Peter was the seminal thinker in the field of management, respected round the world. Who was I to take his time?

The first surprise was Peter's home. He didn't even have an office outside a converted second bedroom in a pleasant but unexceptional suburban home. I almost walked past it and certainly would not have distinguished it from the other unpretentious dwellings on the street if I hadn't had a house number. There were two midsize Japanese cars in the driveway. I rang the door bell, which clanged like a fire station inside. (Peter was hard of hearing.)

After a few seconds, I heard movement inside and a voice that said, "I'm coming. I'm coming." Outgoing mail was crammed into a fire-engine-red oversized mailbox on the wall just beside me on a small porch. The door opened. Peter extended his hand and drew me inside with a warm, "Come in. Come in, Mr. Buford." Very European and gracious. Nobody had called me "Mr. Buford" in years, except when a vice president

of the local bank called to say that I was overdrawn and to ask if I could immediately make a deposit.

But here I was. I was in the inner sanctum. Peter ushered me to a glassed-in porch toward the back of a house that looked over a small swimming pool. I sat down in a creaking circa-1950s wicker chair across from Peter—no desk interfering. Peter said, "Welcome, Mr. Buford. Now what shall we talk about?" There began my face-to-face relationship with the man who was to shape my life, and not just my business life, over the next 23 years.

At that moment, I was in awe. It was an overwhelming feeling, and one that I would never lose.

My relationship with Peter lasted until his death at age 95 in 2005—during which time I saw Peter at least twice a year face to face. He was my teacher, my mentor, my guide. The dedication in my first book, *Halftime*, reads:

This book is dedicated to the two most important

people in my life:

To

Linda,

the woman who has shaped my heart,

and to

Peter Drucker,

the man who formed my mind.

Peter and I were drawn together by common cause: building on the islands of health and strength in what Peter called the social sector. In 1974, after writing his magnum opus, *Management: Tasks, Responsibilities, Practices,* in which he laid down the foundation for the practice of management for business enterprises, Peter began to focus more and more on other forms of organizations, ones that were vital not only to the prosperity but to the nobler purposes of the developed society in which most of us have been fortunate to live during our post-WWII lives. Peter's mission was to create what he came to call a Functioning Society. He called it "The Alternative to Tyranny" in the preface of his big book.

We can all learn from Peter.

Peter was asked in early 1999, "What do you consider to be your most important contribution?" His answer:

"That I early on—almost sixty years ago—realized that management has become the constitutive organ and function of the *Society of Organizations;*

"That management is not 'Business Management'—though it first attained attention in business—but the governing organ of *all* institutions of Modern Society;

"That I established the study of management as a discipline in its own right;

and

"That I focused this discipline on People and Power; on Values, Structure, and Constitution; and above all, on responsibilities—that is, focused the Discipline of Management on management as a truly liberal art."

Peter described himself as a social ecologist. Jim Collins, the man many think of as the leading successor to Drucker, once asked me, over dinner in Dallas, "Do you think Drucker would have been more influential if he had written less?" After a long pause to think, I answered, "No. Peter's mission was to create the platform that all the rest of us are building on." Another management legend, Warren Bennis, put it this way in his endorsement of a book of essays on Peter: "This compilation of smart essays on *The Drucker Difference* illustrates how astonishingly wide the wings of Drucker's wisdom have spread. We all stand gratefully in his shadows, silent in awe."

I, for one, was most interested in applying Peter's ideas to two subsets of the social sector, using management to scale up nonprofit community organizations. My par-

ticular focus was to strengthen the leadership of what are now called mega-churches. Ninety percent of America's population growth in the last several decades has come from the exponential growth of its suburbs. (David Brooks's book, *On Paradise Drive,* offers the best description of this new culture.) Peter was quoted in *Forbes* magazine as saying, "The pastoral mega-churches that have been growing so very fast in the U.S. since 1980 are surely the most important social phenomenon in American society in the last 30 years." As you can imagine, that was a huge encouragement to me and many others.

With Peter's mentorship, I created two organizations to serve the leaders in the social sector. It became my Second Half career. In 1990, Frances Hesselbein, who headed the Girl Scouts of the U.S.A., Dick Schubert, the former head of the American Red Cross, and I co-founded the Peter F. Drucker Foundation for Nonprofit Management (now Leader to Leader Institute at www.leadertoleader.org). It would provide encouragement, leadership training, and, I may say, legitimacy for thousands of well-intentioned but often inadequately managed nonprofit organizations. This publication is one of its projects.

In 1984, I founded another more specialized organization, Leadership Network (www.leadnet.org), to serve the leaders of large churches, a segment that has shown remarkable growth. In 1984, 100 U.S. churches had more than 1,000 in weekly attendance. In 2009, more than 7,000 churches have this attendance. What other phenomenon besides the tech-boom has seen so much growth (with so little media fanfare)? That said, Peter would often caution me, saying, "The purpose of management for the church is not to make the church more businesslike but more churchlike."

In 1995, after several years of conversation with and coaching by Peter, I wrote a book titled *Halftime: Changing Your Game Plan from Success to Significance.* (An updated and expanded version of *Halftime,* with a foreword written by Jim Collins, was released by Zondervan in 2008, along with a book of essays titled *Beyond Halftime.*)

I used my own experience to trace Peter's insight that successful people are not likely to live comfortably in retirement. Their best option is to shift from building their personal portfolios to serving others with their hard-earned skills. To modify slightly the words of Winston Churchill, never, never, never, never quit working.

Peter is now part of my DNA. I hardly recognize any-more which ideas and thoughts have originated in me and which came from Peter's Olympian mind. The author, Jack Beatty, several years ago interviewed me for a book titled *The World According to Peter Drucker*. The interview lasted two hours. Beatty used six of my words: "He's the brains. I'm the legs." It is a near-perfect description.

I want to end by speaking of the specific. A writer from *Inc.* magazine who was doing a piece on mentoring called me with a single question: "What does Peter Drucker do for you as a mentor?" Here, without elaboration, is what I said. It is a guide for all mentors.

What Peter Did for Me as a Mentor

1. He defined the landscape:

   • What's behind, ahead, to each side (the context).

2. He defined the opportunities, the "white space," what is needed *now*.

3. He helped me to clarify my strengths and capacities:

   • To build on strength.

   • To identify the strengths of others that I needed to be effective.

4. He identified the myths, the false paths, the incorrect assumptions of "the industry" within which I was working:

   • What used to be true that no longer is.

   • The conventional wisdom that will lead me astray.

5. He encouraged me to "go for it":

   • He gave me the insight, courage, and confidence to go forward.

6. He helped me to sort out the right strategies.

7. He affirmed results.

8. He pointed out wasted effort:

   • He helped me to *stop* doing things.

9. He (gently) held me accountable.

With the exception of the twelve apostles, I don't think anybody ever had a better mentor. We can all learn from Peter. I miss him deeply.

Bob Buford is chairman of the board of The Buford Foundation/Leadership Network. He is also chairman of The Drucker Institute at Claremont Graduate University. He was the chairman of the board and CEO of Buford Television, Inc., a family-owned business that started with a single ABC affiliate in Tyler, Texas, in the early 1950s, and grew to a network of cable systems across the country. Bob Buford has written four books: "Half Time," "Game Plan," "Stuck in Halftime," and "Finishing Well" (Zondervan). Buford was a co-founder and the initial chairman of the board of The Peter F. Drucker Foundation for Nonprofit Management, now Leader to Leader Institute.

PETER DRUCKER: THE EVER-GIVING LIFE

by Richard Francis Schubert

I t was 1983, just a few months after I'd taken office as president of the American Red Cross. I was near the end of my first swing through some of the largest chapters on the West Coast, and I was flying back to Washington. I was totally absorbed in the job of preserving an already-great reputation and in assessing and addressing a few major issues.

One of those issues had been brought to my attention in a rather inconspicuous way, just two weeks after assuming responsibility, by a small group of top representatives of the organization's Blood Services Unit. The group had given me an extensive briefing a month or so before during a wonderful transition period, as my predecessor was closing out his tenure. They said, "As we were reviewing the briefing notes we realized that we had forgotten one bit of information. We don't think it has anything to do with blood, but you should know about it—it's called Acquired Immune Deficiency Syndrome." The other major issue had to do with money—the organization was in a deficit position and the national office had to reduce staff.

I had gone through my briefcase and at the bottom of my reading pile was a copy of *Across the Board* magazine—the official publication of the Conference Board of America. In it was an article on the greatest management guru of the last 100 years, Peter Drucker. The article referred to Peter's habit of giving time each year to nonprofits. I took out my handheld dictating machine and prepared a note to Peter, indicating that we could use any help he could provide. Peter called the day he received the letter and invited me to come out the next Saturday morning. It was the moment that changed my life.

I actually went out on several consecutive Saturdays and ultimately was a part of the triumvirate who asked Peter for permission to form the Drucker Foundation. The rest is history, as the articles in this special volume of *Leader to Leader* make apparent.

Good intentions are no longer enough.

Peter loved to walk on the trails of the small mountain range behind Claremont College, and that is what we did on those Saturday visits. His approach seldom included direct advice. Rather, he just asked incredibly probing questions that made me think about what we were doing at the Red Cross. There were a couple of memorable exceptions. After hearing about all the organization's programs, he said, "You are trying to do too much." This ultimately led to a critical review of who we really were, our vision and mission, and what we were about, our strategic plan.

Another such moment, after I had told him that we were going to have to cut the national headquarters staff, prompted this reply: "You do not cut your leg off one inch at a time." This led to a resolve to get to a 25 percent reduction as humanely, fairly, and quickly as possible, so we could say to the remaining staff, "We are a team and we can do it."

There were many other special moments with Peter over the years. On one occasion (I think after the Berlin Wall came down, an event he had envisioned), we told him that he had the ability to foretell the future. He replied, "No, I just look out the window at the trends and try to understand what impact they might have." And then, subsequently, he lamented about the lack of window-gazing time for CEOs; the counterproductive business absorption with quarterly earnings; the unacceptable differential between CEO compensation and that of the rest of the workforce—leading to his feeling that CEOs should not be paid more than 20 times their entry-level employees' wage. He also talked about the criticality of water, "the most important commodity in the world"; the incredible challenge of migration from rural areas to cities around the globe; and the performance challenge of NGOs: "Good intentions are no longer enough. There is a bottom line—changed lives." He talked about the challenge to Europe of an uncompetitive economy, the challenge of the Japanese with an aging population, and, of course, the emergence of China. Peter had a way of always making "truth telling" compellingly clear.

My son, David, also had a Peter experience. He had received a master's in microbiology and was searching for some direction with regard to graduate business education. Peter agreed to see David. In David's own words:

"I had the rare privilege of having Peter question all of my assumptions at the literal starting line of my planned career in the biotechnology industry, which at the time was in its infancy and even more risk-laden than today. This several-hour session took place at Peter's kitchen table and included the most prolific management author on the planet making a ham sandwich (on homemade bread made by Peter and Doris) for a know-nothing graduate student. Saying it was surreal is an understatement.

"Of my most prized material possessions is a hand-signed Peter Drucker print that has hung in my office since I graduated from business school. The print lists Peter's mantra:

What is our business?

Who is our customer?

What does our customer consider value?

"In these challenging times Peter's wisdom still shines through, as we all attempt to rebuild our economy based on the fundamental truths Peter put forth more than 50 years ago."

On one of those walks in the earliest days, we had been gone about two hours, then far beyond any easily available help, when a rattlesnake slithered across our path not more than three feet away. Suddenly, my life flashed before me in a *New York Times* headline: "Snake bites Drucker as Red Cross President stands idly by." I was terribly deficient in my first-

Integrity is the most important ingredient of leadership.

organizations or even our own lives have been affected by Peter and his many brilliant disciples. We were all so blessed by every moment in his presence. To God we give praise for Peter and his ever-giving life.

aid upgrading and I made a commitment to do so on my return.

Peter's thinking continues to influence and enlighten us. In fact, when you think about his critiques of executive pay and the obsession with quarterly performance, I can only wish that more organizations were aware of Peter's beliefs. As he often said, "When all is said and done, integrity is the single most important ingredient of leadership." I'm involved in executive coaching and I use this sentence every day.

Finally, there is Peter's generous and gracious spirit, his concern about family challenges and personal faith, never on his sleeve but palpable and actionable in places like the Salvation Army and Catholic charities. All of us involved in the governance or management of

Richard Francis Schubert is executive vice president of Executive Coaching, Inc., and vice chairman of the Leader to Leader Institute. He is chairman of the National Job Corps Association and past president of the American Red Cross. Mr. Schubert was deputy secretary of labor in the Nixon-Ford administration, and is a former president of Bethlehem Steel.

PETER DRUCKER: A GENEROUS SPIRIT

by Michele Hunt

Peter Drucker's groundbreaking contribution to management theory and his impact on thousands of leaders and organizations around the world are unparalleled. This is a personal story about how Peter helped shape my beliefs about leadership and how those beliefs in turn helped build up the companies and institutions I have been privileged to serve.

I feel very fortunate to have had the opportunity to learn from three of the greatest minds (and hearts) of our time: Peter Drucker, Max De Pree, and Frances Hesselbein. These special people are inextricably connected in the web of events and circumstances that helped shape my work and my life. Through their mentorship I was exposed to innovative, enlightened leadership and management philosophies and practices.

Max has been my mentor and dear friend for more than 28 years. (Max De Pree is a former CEO of Herman Miller and the author of the huge best seller *Leadership Is an Art*.) Peter was one of Max's "chief mentors." Max was generous, and he gave the leaders of Herman Miller access to Peter. I took full advantage of this opportunity, and Peter became my mentor as well. It was through Max and Peter that I met Frances Hesselbein, who for the last 20 years has also been my mentor and dear friend. In Max's monograph *The Gift of Mentoring,* he says of his three chief mentors: "Their mentoring—I would almost rather say their ministering—in my life has been absolutely critical to my development as a leader and to the quality of my family's life." I feel the same and am deeply grateful for these gifts. The cumulative effect of these three people had a profound impact on what I believe, who I have become, and the contribution I have been able to make through my work—a beautiful cycle.

The Magic of Herman Miller

I first met Peter in 1986, when I was vice president *for* people at Herman Miller. We were facing tremendous challenges. After decades of success we were becoming irrelevant. We learned the hard way that nothing fails like success. We had become complacent and developed a touch of arrogance—a very dangerous place to be. We were isolated and insulated from the changes occurring in the world around us, out of touch with our customers, the changing workforce, and changes in the environment. Most damaging, we got off mission. We had grown so fast that we had neglected to communicate a clear direction to our employees. We also had failed to pass on the company values. When we were small, we could share the vision and values through stories and relationships, but we had become large and complex—we had lost our way. The consequences would have been dire if we had not changed. Max called for a companywide renewal. We struggled with Peter's five most important questions:

- What is our mission?

- Who is our customer?

- What does our customer value?

- What are our results?

- What is our plan?

We renewed our mission, created a *shared* vision, and clarified our core values. We accomplished this in a unique manner. We created a disciplined process that genuinely engaged every work team and every individual in the company.

The results were amazing! All the employees wanted the same thing—to reclaim our leadership position. Our vision became: "To Be a Reference Point for Quality and Excellence." Max then asked a very important question: "What values do we need to

Nothing fails like success.

embrace and build into the organization to become a reference point for quality and excellence?" Once again we went to the people. After hearing their input we settled on seven core values that would guide everyone's decisions and behaviors:

- Customer-focused vision: Put the customer at the center of our vision.

- Participation and teamwork: Recognize the value and collective genius of people. People have the right and responsibility to contribute their gifts.

- Ownership: Treat employees like owners. Grant them stock and allow everyone to be responsible and accountable for the decisions that affect their work. Employee-owners have a right to share in the risk and rewards of the business.

- Valuing uniqueness: Encourage people to bring their whole self to work and to contribute their uniqueness to help achieve the company's goals. Value differences and celebrate the richness of diversity.

- Family, social, and environmental responsibility: Work, family, and communities are inextricably connected. Our management decisions should aim for innovative solutions that would not harm these important stakeholders.

- Become a learning organization: Invest in developing employees, leaders, and teams. Continual learning is a shared commitment.

- Financial soundness: While essential, it is not the single aim of our work. It is the result of our commitment to our mission, vision, values, and goals, and our collective efforts.

The leadership team looked at the vision and values and realized how big and bold they were. This led us to struggle with some very serious questions:

- Is it possible to achieve such lofty goals?

- Are the vision and values appropriate for a public company?

- In light of our economic challenges—do we have the time and resources to do this?

We concluded that we must. We had to renew the company and we needed everyone's help. We found the courage to align everything to serve our mission, vision, values, and goals. Working in cross-level, cross-functional teams, we aligned our strategies, structures, systems, policies, communications, recognition, and rewards—and most important, our leadership decisions and behaviors. Within eighteen months, Herman Miller went from near failure to these heights:

- Fortune's Most Admired Company

- Best Products by Business Week

- One of the 10 Best Companies to Work For

- Best Company for Women

- Best Company for Working Mothers

- Numerous environmental awards, including the White House Presidential Citation for being one of the nation's 10 most environmentally responsible corporations

- The Best Managed Company in the world—the Bertelsmann Foundation

At the same time, sales increased 20 percent. We returned to double-digit growth. Employee-owners contributed more than $12 million in cost savings per year.

It was an exciting time at Herman Miller. People all over the company were working together creating the future. The excitement was palpable.

Peter Drucker's beliefs and philosophy were a part of this transformation. We transformed the company into what Peter called a "responsibility-based organization." We came to embody the three critical elements Peter describes as necessary for this kind of organization:

- *Move from command to information:* We held monthly business reviews to share information (the good, the bad, and the ugly) with *all* work teams. Collaboration rather than hierarchy drove the organization. Everyone knew the corporate goals and priorities, and everyone knew the status of our progress. This enabled the work teams to celebrate the good news and to put a laser focus on the problem areas. This also required that everyone become business literate, so we provided education on the fundamentals of business for all employees.

- *Move from information to responsibility:* All work teams were responsible for the company's key goals. Each team created its own goals in support of the company's overarching goals. They were responsible and accountable for their performance. Unlike most companies, which reward only executives, at Herman Miller everyone from the janitor to the CEO shared in a company-wide quarterly bonus called "Our Earned Share," awarded when we outperformed our corporate goals. People rarely let us down, and often they exceeded our expectations. They did not act as subordinates or employees—they acted like owners, or what Peter called "responsible decision makers."

- *Make everyone a contributor:* People were liberated to contribute their talents beyond the traditional boundaries found in most organizations. You never heard someone say, "That's not my job." People contributed innovative ideas that greatly improved every aspect of the business.

The key ingredient was our commitment to lead people differently. Many of us had to change our basic beliefs about leadership. Max taught us that leadership was a function and not a status, or as

Peter put it, "Rank does not confer privilege or give power, it imposes responsibility." Our role was one of servant leadership. Max commissioned a sculpture of a water carrier. It was placed in the courtyard of the Corporate Center to remind us that our job was to enable people to serve the company's mission, vision, values, and goals. Our vision served as our North Star, and our values became our rudder as we transformed ourselves.

For many of us, Herman Miller was Camelot! Peter's wise insights helped shape who and what we became. Peter was right: "The best way to predict the future is to create it."

Reinventing Government

I took what I learned from Peter and Max and the Herman Miller experience to work on one of the toughest jobs one can imagine—reinventing the U.S. government. I was appointed by President Clinton to serve as director of the Federal Quality Institute. Its mandate was to help create a government that worked better and cost less. The institute's mission was to bring the most effective and efficient leadership and management philosophies and practices to U.S. government leaders, to enable them to reinvent themselves. Through public-private partnerships, the best leaders in business contributed their time and experience.

When I called Peter for help, he immediately responded, "Yes, of course." He became my trusted handholder and friend. His counsel was priceless. He not only was the pioneer of modern management, he had also advised many U.S. presidents, starting with President Truman, and worked on many government initiatives. Peter understood the federal government's complex and convoluted environment. He had experienced firsthand the tremendous resistance to change and the cynical attitudes of people in and outside government. Knowing this, Peter believed that working to make government more effective and efficient was critically important to sustaining our democracy.

Rank imposes responsibility.

On one occasion I had the honor of facilitating a videoconference with Peter and the leadership teams of the agencies. He gave some very important advice:

- Revisit your mission. Make sure it is not based on outdated assumptions.

- Always look at what is working first. Celebrate and build on your strengths.

- Look at what you need to do differently.

- Create across-the-board standards and goals.

- Create an institutional habit of continuous improvement.

- Service, efficiency, and making life simpler for your customers should be your goal.

- Value your employees. Employees are the best PR for any organization.

(*Note:* A DVD of this interview is available through Leader to Leader Institute and at www.dreammakers.org.)

Peter's advice applies to organizations in all sectors and transcends time.

Our Legacy, Our Time

Over the past thirteen years, I have worked as a change catalyst, bringing Peter's wise insights and the Herman Miller experience to leadership teams that strive to "do good and do well." I have seen the power of this form of leadership—the tangible results *and* the joy, excitement, and pride it generates in people. I believe it is not just *possible* to become what Peter calls a responsibility-based organization, but that it is *necessary* for our society to survive and thrive.

Now it's our time to rethink how we lead our organizations, communities, and institutions. Nothing seems to be working. Every institution that guided us and served as our compass in the past is struggling with its identity and survival. The proliferation of economic, political, social, and environmental crises across our world is staggering. We are living in an unprecedented time of global change.

Peter describes this time as "The Great Divide."

"Every few years in Western history, there occurs a sharp transformation. We cross a divide. Within a few short decades, society rearranges itself; its basic views; its social and political structure; its arts; its key institutions. Fifty years later there is a new world. And people born then cannot even imagine the world in which their grandparents lived, and into which their parents were born."

We are living through such a great divide. However, change is happening so fast that we are seeing the new world unfold very rapidly. *How* our world unfolds will depend on us! How we see our world and the decisions we make now are powerfully shaping our future. This is a defining moment in the history of humankind. We have compelling reasons to become a *responsibility-based* society. A whole new level of responsibility and accountability is required of us all.

Throughout history we have been given a glimpse of greatness—great thinkers and great leaders.

Peter was one of the greats! The generative impact of Peter's contribution is powerful. He has profoundly touched the lives of thousands of leaders and organizations through his work and his mentorship. He passed his insights on to Max. Max integrated Peter's ideas and put them to work at Herman Miller. The cumulative effect of Peter's work is incalculable.

The world needs leaders with a purpose that transcends corporate selfishness.

Now more than ever we need leaders to teach and demonstrate the power of ethical leadership. We need leaders who understand that to serve is an honorable goal, and who have a deep and abiding respect for *all* people. The world needs leaders with a purpose that transcends corporate selfishness, individual materialism, and the seduction of power. We need leaders who understand the myriad connections both among and within individuals, families, organizations, communities, and the environment. Now is the time for leaders with the faith and courage to hold a positive vision for the future and the heart to love and respect what it means to be human in a world that increasingly appears to be broken.

The global crises of our time may be a gift. As I move around the world, I see that there is almost universal agreement that fundamental change is needed. People are yearning for healthier, lighter, more meaningful ways of working and being. They are asking very important questions:

- The global crises of our time may be a gift. What is important to me?

- How do I find meaning in life?

- How do I want to spend the rest of my life?

Most important, something deeply profound is happening. From the growing level of discontent, something beautiful is emerging. A shift in consciousness is rippling across our world, awakening a sense of spirit and a growing desire to express that spirit in our work, institutions, communities, and personal lives. To bring that spirit to life, we need leaders who find the courage to ask some very personal and important questions:

- What is my responsibility?

- Who am I accountable to?

- Am I worthy to lead?

- Can I create places worthy of people's commitment?

- What do I want my legacy to be?

It is time we become what Peter called "responsible decision makers" and align our actions with our aspirations to create a new and better world—a world where the divine spirit in all of us is allowed to flourish.

Michele Hunt is a Change Catalyst and "Thinking Partner" to leaders on leadership development, and organizational transformation and effectiveness. She is a speaker and the author of "DreamMakers: Putting Vision & Values to Work." In 1993, she was appointed by President Clinton as director of the Federal Quality Institute, a part of the Reinventing Government initiative. She previously served on the senior management team of Herman Miller as corporate vice president for people, with responsibility for leadership development, human resources, quality, and communications.

WHAT PETER DRUCKER'S FOUR GREAT LESSONS TAUGHT US TO DO

by T. George Harris and Craig B. Wynett

In describing what we learned from Peter Drucker, it's automatic to assume that our relationship fit traditional teacher-student stereotypes. However, while we may have been typical students, Peter Drucker was most definitely not a typical teacher.

As a team, our relationship with Peter began to gather momentum in early 1993. (Harris by this time was already a lifelong Drucker protégé. In fact, he was the one who had persuaded Peter to move west from NYU to become distinguished professor at Claremont Graduate School.) Wynett, having been assigned to restart P&G's long-dormant Corporate New Ventures program, teamed with Harris to bring Peter in to gather up a few how-to tips on innovation.

To our delight, things did not go according to plan.

To begin with, there were no how-to tips. Nor was there the typical one-way flow of information from wise teacher to naive student. Peter was not about to let us off that easy. "You won't learn anything from me unless I learn something from you," he said. And so began an intense relationship that lasted right up to his death in 2005.

Peter always had a good story to tell—Peter's Parables, we called them. They sometimes seemed to wander off the subject until we'd suddenly realize that he had just reinvented reality. He never failed to keep us in gales of laughter as he recounted the trials and triumphs of literally hundreds of organizations he'd guided and studied since the 1920s. Part of Peter's genius was his ability to give an insider's account of business by applying the rigorous concepts of academic thought. Here are a few highlights from our 12-year apprenticeship with the architect of modern management:

Lesson 1:

Unprecedented change is a time to reexamine basic assumptions.

One of Peter's most important lessons was perhaps the most basic: "Assumptions matter." Accurate assumptions are the fundamental requirement for developing winning strategies. But, as he pointed out, the most crucial of these assumptions are the ones so taken for granted that they are barely visible . . . after a while the fish no longer notices the water. For most, the reality of how central water is in everyday life goes largely unappreciated right up to the moment when the lake dries up. Peter's suggestion, delivered with his deep Austrian accent: "Don't become a fish out of water." And how do you change these invisible rules? You make them visible.

In business, the most basic assumptions are rooted in the belief that bigger is not only better, and that it is the only viable option. And for most of the 20th century, this assumption was shared by many.

Historically, the inefficiencies of the global market created by distance, differing regulatory requirements, language barriers, communication gaps, and the like generated a dynamic in which companies found that they could build most capabilities themselves far more cheaply than it would cost to hire or buy those same capabilities on the outside. This explains why companies like General Motors, IBM, General Electric, and so on grew so large—they internalized more and more market functions over an ever-wider range of activities. The total quality movement (TQM) was an inevitable result of the need to make a large and growing asset base of plant and equipment as efficient as possible. And as Peter helped us understand, powerful forces of the last half century were coming together in a crescendo of change.

To our delight, things did not go according to plan.

As Peter saw it, the last two decades of the 20th century were years of unprecedented change. The combination of deregulation, the increasing mobility of capital, the IT revolution, and the consolidation of global standards was beginning to have a decisive impact. As well, the Internet was clearly making the world a much smaller place. As a result, falling transaction costs were reducing the advantages that big business once exercised over labor, markets, capital, and distribution channels.

In this seriously changed environment, corporate competencies that once gave us cost and value advantages were becoming core rigidities that began to drive up costs, limit flexibility, and offer less and less incremental benefits beyond their free-market counterparts. As Peter saw it, "It may be precisely the very perfection of the current system that has become a straitjacket. It has made the system rigid. And it tends to imprison the individual's knowledge in the silo of a specialty, a brand, a market segment, rather than allow it to become a company asset."

So the question became, If the old, easily imitated sources of competitive advantage were losing their edge, then what are the new sources? For Peter Drucker, the answer was simple: "P&G has achieved its preeminence by creating a franchise. It now needs to build its success on enriching the yield from the franchise. That means increasing, by several magnitudes—the productivity of the one capital asset in which P&G already has a decided advantage and a superior record: performing people."

Where do big ideas come from?

Lesson 2:

Human creativity will replace economies of scale as the chief source of competitive advantage in the 21st-century corporation.

Most companies have long since pushed mergers and acquisitions to the limit. They have also realized that the benefits of reengineering and downsizing are no substitute for policies that lead to sustained, profitable growth. Peter felt that most CEOs had at last come to the sane conclusion that innovation is the only durable touchstone for healthy growth. So it has always been, but in today's competitive world it's become so obvious that any organization unable to find and nurture creative talent is in serious trouble. But unlike the transparency of TQM, the thought processes involved in producing breakthrough innovations are less obvious, and for many, even mysterious.

This lack of transparency has led to the common belief that creativity is more like a genetic gift than a teachable skill. But is it? Is it really a rare gift of a select few (Da Vinci, Mozart), or is it a skill we all possess to some degree, like athleticism, and can improve with practice? For Peter, these were crucial business questions. Their answers determined whether we as managers can substantially improve the creative process that drives innovation.

Whether creativity lives inside the many or just the few is a fundamental question for anybody who thinks for a living. If game-changing ideas arise mainly through the inspired, unpredictable flashes of a maverick genius, then the role of the manager is very limited. The job is reduced to one of being a cheerleader. Round up all the gifted people and then get out of their way while they work their magic. If, on the other hand, creativity turns out to be a trainable skill, then the manager's role is truly significant. Peter, clearly knowing the answer, told us to find out for ourselves whether an organization's creative capacity was due to nature, nurture, or a combination of both.

Lesson 3:

Creativity is an activity, not a gift.

Calling creativity "the fuzzy front-end," business has tended to treat it more as alchemy than chemistry—a seemingly magical process that has the power to turn lead into gold, a small idea into a gigantic discontinuity. The alchemists were attempting to investigate nature before basic scientific tools were available, relying on folklore and mysticism to fill in the gaps. However, when new technology allowed scientists to see more clearly into the core of molecules, alchemy lost its appeal. Peter made sure we understood that we were at this same point in the scientific study of creativity. Today, cognitive scientists have brought us to a point where we can start using rigorously studied principles of human thought to enhance our own creative potential as well as that of our colleagues.

As creativity continues to reveal itself as a generally predictable and controllable process, it now seems clear that building a highly innovative organization requires a scientifically based understanding of how individuals and groups develop breakthrough ideas. Peter posed a simple question: "Where do big ideas come from? Or for that matter," he added, "where does any idea come from?"

Despite the fact that many innovators report that their big idea just seemed to pop into mind, such original thinking simply cannot be conceived out of thin air. The brain is left to produce even the most radical ideas out of what it already has on hand—existing knowledge. The cognitive process responsible for the recycling of old knowledge into new ideas is analogy—pattern recognition by an experienced mind, which transforms a memory into a creative new insight.

Lesson 4:

Management practices developed to drive ever-greater productivity out of physical assets tend to backfire when aimed at increasing the creative productivity of knowledge workers.

Indeed, the primary tools of the traditional manager were developed in a time in which employees were treated as a cost—something to be minimized and rendered routine. Peter told us, "Traditionally, companies focused on optimizing market capital—brands—and treated the information, knowledge, and passion of people as an 'input,' that is, the traditional economist's 'labor,' and a 'cost,' rather than considering the information, knowledge, and passion of performing people as 'intellectual capital.'" The goal of command-and-control management was efficiency.

As Peter pointed out, the TQM mantra—simplify, standardize, make identical—while essential for driving ever greater levels of productivity from physical assets, seemed to have the exact opposite effect on human knowledge workers, namely, driving them to ever lower levels of creativity and innovation. Using motivational tools like incentive pay as the carrot and the threat of firing as the stick, these approaches were designed to encourage people to do the same thing over and over, more reliably, and faster. But these "extrinsic" motivators by themselves do not provide the basis for a highly entrepreneurial workforce. According to Peter, "It does not utilize (or only marginally) the individual's motivation and passion, the 'fire in the belly.' This means that performance standards are *minimums,* below which the individual is not allowed to fall. The exceptional performer does so despite them rather than because of them." Innovation, unlike productivity, cannot simply be ordered up. For anybody to innovate, the motive has to come from the inside, stimulated by intrinsic rather than extrinsic rewards, drawing motivation and satisfaction from the excitement in the job itself.

To create and sustain an innovative culture, you have to go beyond being managers to become lead-

To innovate, the motive has to come from inside.

ers, perhaps what can be marked as *intrinsic leaders.* Leaders seek out the inner passions of the people who work with them—and the managers above, below, sideways—and liberate the energy of their imagination. Leaders help people know how to trust their informed gut instinct. ("I can do no other," Martin Luther said in launching his reformation against another hierarchy.) Leaders fire the vision and encourage people to pursue new knowledge resources and alliances across the silos of isolated disciplines.

In a few hundred years, when the history of our time will be written, it is likely that historians will not see the technology explosion, the Internet, or e-commerce as the most important developments of the late twentieth and early twenty-first centuries. Rather, it will be the unprecedented advance in the human condition. In spite of global wars and holocausts, there is now an irreversible trend toward longer, better lives and greater freedom. For the first time—literally—substantial and rapidly growing numbers of people have choices not only about food and health but also about how they can make their lives and work meaningful. For the first time, employees who were once Organization Men and Women have to manage their lives not just to be successful but also to be significant.

No one labored so long and wisely as Drucker to encourage each new step toward decent bossing, honest marketing, entrepreneurial innovation, and the full development of each individual's talents regardless of race, gender, or faith. From Japan and China to South Africa and Mexico, the common language of dedicated leadership generally comes from this immigrant American, our friend, the late Peter F. Drucker. Arguably, he has done more than any other thinker to shape the organizations of our age, and help others find their way toward healthier, fuller lives, blessed by the thrill of serving others.

T. George Harris, a legendary magazine editor, is the founder and former editor-in-chief of American Health; he is also a former editor-in-chief of Psychology Today and The Harvard Business Review. Under his leadership, Psychology Today and American Health received the American Society of Magazine Editors Magazine of the Year award. He was the first editor to be selected for two different magazines.

Craig B. Wynett is the chief creative officer of Procter & Gamble and has played a leading role in revitalizing P&G's innovation efforts. This includes the development of P&G's Corporate New Ventures department, which has been responsible for creating many of P&G's most successful new products, including Swiffer.

CRAFTING A CULTURE OF CHARACTER

by C. William Pollard

During my leadership years at ServiceMaster and thereafter, Peter Drucker was a valued adviser, mentor, and friend. The lessons learned were many. Our friendship grew to include his wife, Doris. The two of them were a team, a partnership that often provided me with a lesson by example of the importance of continuing to nurture a partnership with my wife, Judy.

As I look back on my relationship with Peter, I realize how deeply he shaped my thinking and contributed to the person I have become. I grew to understand my strengths and weaknesses and how I could be more effective as I led, served, and worked with others.

During the time that I led ServiceMaster, Peter influenced my thinking in four areas:

Planning

The only thing certain about tomorrow is that it will be different from today.

—Peter Drucker

During most of my leadership years at ServiceMaster, we grew at a compounded rate of 20 percent per year. Planning and change were a way of life for us, and with Peter's help, we were able to focus on those strategic issues that would influence our future. He would often remind us that long-range planning was more of a process than a result. The more people we involved in the process, the better we would prepare them for those changes that would inevitably occur in the future.

During a period when we were wrestling with declining growth in one of our major business units and were considering several new market opportunities, I asked Peter to come and speak to our board of directors about planning for the future.

He first asked the board one of his own famous questions, "What is your business?" After listening to board members respond by telling him what markets we served and what services we provided to those markets, he said, "You're all wrong."

Abandon yesterday's heroes.

He went on to tell them that, in his judgment, our business was simply the training and development of people. We packaged our services in different ways to meet the needs and demands of our customers. But we couldn't deliver services without people—we couldn't deliver quality services without trained and motivated people who were also happy in their work.

These statements were all consistent with one of our company objectives: "To help people develop." Peter was emphasizing that this had become a core competency and that we needed to recognize it as such. It was a foundational strength that should determine which new and growing markets we should enter. It was an important lesson, one that for some may be simple—but for us at that time it was profound. It provided the guidance and direction for our decision to expand some of our existing services and to acquire and develop new services for the consumer market. This market would later become the major growth engine for ServiceMaster, as we came to provide more than 10 million homeowners with one or more of our services.

Leadership

> Leadership is just a means—to what end is the real question?
>
> —*Peter Drucker*

In my discussions with Peter on leadership he would always emphasize the importance of the leader's responsibility to the people being led. Leaders needed to know what they believed and why they believed it, and where they were going and why it was important for people to follow. People needed leadership that they could trust—leadership that would nurture their souls.

Peter never hesitated to point out those areas where I could improve my leadership. One of those important moments of learning occurred when we were traveling together to conduct a management seminar in Tokyo for Japanese business leaders.

After the seminar, Peter and I had dinner. I shared with him my disappointment, and yes, even anger, over the fact that no one from the leadership team of our Japanese business partner had come to the seminar. They had been invited and had promised to attend. Since some of our current and prospective customers were in attendance, it would have provided an opportunity for them to learn and also to make important business connections.

I explained to Peter that we had recently decided to delay bringing one of our new service lines to Japan and that our partner was upset with that decision. I explained that this was probably the reason its leaders did not come.

I told Peter that I intended to cancel my trip to their headquarters in Osaka and take an earlier flight back to the States. Peter encouraged me to rethink my position and gave some advice, including his thoughts and understanding of Japanese culture. Although I listened to him, I made up my mind that I was not going to accept his advice and I would reschedule my flight the next morning.

When dinner was over we returned to our respective hotel rooms. At about 10:30 that evening, I received a call from Peter asking me if I would come to his room. He was still concerned about my reactions and wanted a further discussion with me.

As Peter opened the door to his hotel room, I could tell by the look on his face that he was troubled. He told me to sit on the chair near his bed. He then sat down on the edge of his bed and looked me straight in the eye. "Bill," he said, "you are suffering from the arrogance of success. It's time for you to eat some humble pie." He went on to explain how

If a thing is worth doing, it is worth doing poorly to begin with.

quickly leaders can lose touch with the reality of their responsibility when they think their pride is at risk. He pointed out that my job as leader was to go to Osaka, meet with our business partners, resolve our differences, and rebuild a relationship of trust. This result was needed for the continued growth of our business in Japan and for the opportunities it would provide the people in our business. It was my job to do this as a leader, and it was something that I could not delegate.

It was great advice. The next morning I was on the train to Osaka, and my meeting there accomplished the right result for our business and for our people. I did have to eat some humble pie. The leadership lesson was clear. My leadership responsibility was not about me or my feelings. It was about what should be done for our business and our people.

Innovation

> Innovation is a change which creates a new dimension of performance.
>
> —*Peter Drucker*

As our business grew and became part of that select group, the Fortune 500, Peter would often remind me that organizational structure and size can get in the way of the entrepreneurial spirit and innovation that are essential for the vitality and growth of the firm. He would keep pressing me to focus and feed the breadwinners of tomorrow and abandon yesterday's heroes.

Many of our best innovations and ideas for improving existing services and adding new services and new market opportunities would come from the frontline managers who were close to the customer and who saw opportunities for change that would create a new dimension of performance. Peter helped me to think about how we could change, redefine, and flatten our organizational structure so that the people with the knowledge and information of what the customer needed or wanted were enabled to bring their ideas and innovations forward.

With Peter's help, we learned these important lessons:

- Keeping the organization open and flexible is a never-ending task.

- The potential for the new always requires testing and piloting. If a thing is worth doing, it is worth doing poorly to begin with, so get started and learn from experience.

- Innovators must have elbow room for mistakes but also must be accountable and at risk for the results. No firm can afford to have innovative bystanders.

- You must have an organizational structure that separates the innovative initiative from the main business and protects the new idea from the crushing wheel of the firm's operations.

- You must have supportive senior leadership that is ready to serve and listen, but that also has the discipline to bury the dead. It is hard for a successful firm to accept failure, but in Drucker's words, "The corpse doesn't smell any better the longer you keep it around."

Mission

> People work for a cause, not just a living.
>
> —*Peter Drucker*

Among the unique characteristics of ServiceMaster that attracted Peter were our corporate objectives:

Leadership starts with the ability to define reality.

To honor God in all we do, To help people develop, To pursue excellence, and To grow profitability. The first two objectives were "end" goals. The second two objectives were "means" goals. We did not use our first objective as a basis for exclusion. It was in fact the reason we promoted diversity, as we recognized that different people with different beliefs were all part of God's mix.

While some may question whether our first objective, to honor God, should be a part of a corporation's mission statement, everyone at ServiceMaster understood and embraced what would happen as a result. That was to recognize the dignity and worth of every person and to accept responsibility for being involved in not only what each person was doing at work, but also the kind of person each was becoming.

Peter's classic definition of management is getting the right things done through others. But he doesn't stop there. In his concept of management as a liberal art, he also suggests that a manager must be concerned about what is happening to the person in the process. Those people who are producing the profits, and the products and services of the firm, are also human. They have cares and concerns, emotions and feelings, beliefs and convictions. They have the potential to do good or evil, to love or hate, contribute or detract, motivate or discourage. Thus, as we manage and lead we should seek to understand the nature of their humanity, including the spiritual dimension of the human condition.

Peter would frequently remind me that this dimension of management was about character development and was consistent with the way that ServiceMaster was implementing its objectives. We were a successful business but we were also seeking to be a moral community for the development of human character. As such, we performed an important social function, one that went beyond providing society with needed goods and services. We were, in his terms, human change agents as we addressed the question of what people were becoming in the work environment, not just what they were doing.

My dialogues with Peter on this subject were special learning experiences for me, as he shared the background and development of his thinking on the role of the corporation in society and the function of the organization as an instrument of human achievement, human growth, and human fulfillment. His thoughts about the nature of human existence and the importance of faith are described in his essay "The Unfashionable Kierkegaard."

As our discussions on this subject continued over time, Peter prodded me to recognize and accept the responsibility to promote the idea of the business firm as a moral community, not only within the walls of ServiceMaster but beyond. He suggested that I should be writing a book and speaking about it in various venues, including graduate schools of business.

Peter was suggesting a new mission for my life and work beyond being the CEO at ServiceMaster, a mission that would develop into an organizing principle for how I could share my philosophy of life and work with others.

There would be much for me to learn in this expanded role that Peter had envisioned. Writing a book would definitely be beyond my comfort zone.

But with Peter's help the book, *The Soul of the Firm,* was written—and it turned out to be a best seller. He also helped design a lecture series for graduate schools of business, a series that would focus on the source of moral authority and ethical behavior in business. And over the years there have been many opportunities for me to speak and teach on the subject. It was Peter as the social ecologist who provided much of my learning and inspiration for this new phase of my life.

As I reflect on some of the issues we are currently dealing with in our economy, issues that were caused in part by leadership that focused only on the profit motive and short-term gains, I realize there is still much to be done to carry on Peter's legacy.

Effective, responsible leadership starts with the ability of a leader to define reality, and to understand the essence of one's own human nature and the human nature of the people one is leading. Crafting a culture of character requires executives to possess strong moral fiber and to know the source of their moral authority.

C. William Pollard is a former chairman and a two-time CEO of ServiceMaster. He is currently a director of Herman Miller and a number of charitable, religious, and educational organizations, including the Illinois Children's Healthcare Foundation, The Drucker Institute, and the Billy Graham Evangelistic Association. He is the author of the best-selling book, "The Soul of the Firm," and the recently released "Serving Two Masters? Reflections on God and Profit."

THE IMPORTANCE OF INTEGRITY IN A LEADER AND PERSONAL RELATIONSHIPS

by Joseph A. Maciariello

I became aware of Peter Drucker's ideas in 1962, right after graduating from Bryant College in Providence, Rhode Island, with a bachelor's degree in management. My primary professor at Bryant, John McCabe, had a teaching philosophy that sought to convert information into knowledge by having his students write exams that required both mastery of the subject and successful application of the principles of management to specific management problems. He sought understanding, not repetition of information. It was therefore natural for me, when I was trying to solve problems in my first job, at Hamilton Standard, to study Peter Drucker's 1954 book, *The Practice of Management*. Drucker was the first to codify the principles of management, and I tried to apply them to our problems at Hamilton Standard in exactly the way Professor McCabe had taught me.

My mentor, colleague, and friend at Union College in Schenectady, New York, Professor Alfred L. Thimm, referred to Drucker often in his graduate classes. He taught an extraordinary course titled "Advanced Management Theory" in which he assigned a term paper requiring a comparative analysis of the field's four major schools of thought. The paper had to be completed by summer's end, 1966. Major writers covered were Herbert Simon of Carnegie-Mellon, from the Decision-Making School; Jay Forrester of MIT, from the Systems School; Elton Mayo of Harvard, from the Human Relations School; and Peter Drucker of NYU, from the Rational School. Thimm was committed to all four schools of management, but having studied under Peter Drucker, a fellow

Management is a human activity.

Austrian, during his own doctoral work at NYU, he had a deep appreciation of Drucker's contributions to the field.

Thimm encouraged me to go on for my Ph.D. and to do so at NYU. To assist, he offered me a part-time teaching position at Union, beginning in the fall of 1967. I accepted his kind offer and attended NYU, while teaching part-time at Union's program at Vassar College in Poughkeepsie, New York.

Union's graduate program in industrial administration was very demanding, requiring the successful completion of a comprehensive examination at the end of the program of studies, as well as a master's thesis. These requirements were somewhat similar to the requirements of doctoral programs in management at the time. As a result, I decided to pursue my Ph.D. in economics, not in management. I was therefore unable to secure a seat in Drucker's very popular general management course at NYU, since the business school was then at 100 Trinity Place, and Drucker's course was in a room with limited seating capacity.

Right after my graduation from NYU in 1973, my wife, knowing of my interest in management and in Drucker's writings, purchased his new book, *Management: Tasks, Responsibilities, Practices.* From then on, this book played a central role in my life. It is a comprehensive treatment of the entire subject of management and a distillation of all of Drucker's work in management to that point. It is a very mature book, requiring deep experience on the part of the reader to absorb and internalize Drucker's ideas. I spent over three decades mastering those ideas.

When I had the opportunity to join the faculty at Claremont, I accepted largely because of Peter Drucker, although it meant leaving Union College, a school that had helped launch my career, and a school that I still love. My mentor, Alfred Thimm, was disappointed by my move but ultimately agreed with my decision.

One of my major field examinations at NYU was on the works of John Maynard Keynes. When I later found out that Drucker had attended the Keynesian seminars in Cambridge, England, during the time Keynes was writing his *General Theory of Employment, Interest and Money,* I immediately became curious about Drucker's relationship to Keynes' work and to economics. When I discovered that he left the Keynesian seminars in 1934, realizing (as he wrote in *The Ecological Vision*) that "Keynes and all the brilliant economics students in the room were interested in the behavior of commodities . . . while I was interested in the behavior of people," I knew immediately that his reaction to Keynesian economics was similar to mine. Furthermore, his belief that "management is a human activity" resonated deeply. So I wanted very much to learn more about the man, his person, and his works. For the next 26 years he gave me many opportunities to do so.

In 1981, I audited his small Ph.D. seminar in management at Claremont. The text for the course was *Management: Tasks, Responsibilities, Practices.* After the class I started a systematic comparative study of this book in relation to his earlier book, *The Practice of Management,* noting what he kept in, what he left out, and what he added. I began asking him questions about numerous management topics. I always attended his public talks and listened carefully, trying to relate his talks to his writings. It amazed me how he would apply a thought he expressed in his book to the topic he was then addressing. I concluded that his ideas were deep expressions of his beliefs. I began to see the connections between his *beliefs,* his *writings,* and his *behavior.* They were consistent. The man was *authentic,* a person of *integrity.* This is the most important lesson I learned from Peter Drucker.

He said in various places that integrity is "the touchstone" of management. What did he mean? Merriam-

Brilliance in executive leadership is highly overrated.

Webster's dictionary defines *touchstone* as "a test or criterion for determining the quality or genuineness of a thing." Drucker thus taught that the effectiveness of executive leadership is determined by the integrity of the leader. So I began to observe Peter as he exhibited integrity. Most of what I observed was the way he interacted with me and with other people. I will never forget his treatment of me and the lessons I learned. It was like being mentored in character traits, in integrity.

Peter Drucker cared deeply about people. After almost each appointment, my ophthalmologist tells me a "Drucker story" of how Drucker, a family friend, often visited his home for dinner when he was a boy. At each visit, Drucker would ask about the young man, how he was doing, and what he was planning for his life, not in merely a polite way, but in a way that revealed that he really cared and wanted to know.

When I was ill for a long period, Drucker always asked me how I was doing. He called me after a major surgery. To hear from Peter Drucker and to have the sense that he really cared and was trying to cheer me up was encouraging. At the height of my illness, he listened to what was going on and tried to comfort me. At a social gathering he asked my wife how I was getting along. She told him, with considerable irritation, that all I wanted to do was work. And then, surprisingly, Drucker responded to my wife, "And Judy, don't you ever try to stop him." He knew that the work I loved would help keep my mind off the illness and would, in and of itself, help the healing process. Once I started to heal, he noticed it in the way that I was carrying

myself and he commented on it. Drucker was an astute observer of human behavior, always watching.

I learned the importance of manners from Peter Drucker. He frequently wrote notes and made phone calls to thank people who had done things to show him kindness. Manners, he taught, are the lubricant of organizations. He practiced excellent manners in his life.

In the last five years of his life, I had the opportunity to work directly with him. First, I worked on a number of Executive Internet Modules and then on *The Daily Drucker* and *The Effective Executive in Action.* He set very high standards of workmanship, standards I tried to meet. He was refining my personality, extending my vision of what I could do, and giving me a chance to try, although I did fail at times. During the process, I was once accused by an outside party of violating Drucker's standards of integrity. When made aware of this, I stopped all work and faxed Peter a letter, explaining that the incident never happened as reported. Moreover, I told him I did not care about the project, but I did care about my relationship with him. It was a watershed experience because through my actions I believe he came to see that I recognized the importance of integrity in personal relationships, as he taught and modeled. I think my actions at that time assured him that I would never knowingly violate the trust he placed in me.

I began to understand Peter's statement that brilliance in executive leadership is highly overrated. While extremely helpful, it cannot overcome a lack of integrity in a leader because a lack of integrity destroys people, an organization's most valuable resource. I witnessed, on a few occasions, Peter verbally assailing brilliant people who had demonstrated a lack of integrity in their behavior. As I left one such meeting, I said to him, "If I have to leave Claremont today, it would have been worth it to have known you." He said, "Oh, save it until they have thrown dirt over me." I have saved it until now.

Perhaps the most moving experience of my time with Peter Drucker came in December of 2001. Our son, Patrick, had worked with me during his college years,

When in doubt, don't.

researching Drucker's work as it related to my various research projects. He thought he knew Drucker pretty well ("Druckered-out" was the term he used), so when it came time to attend graduate school, he chose to attend Columbia University. When Patrick attended MBA events with senior executives who were visiting Columbia, he was surprised that a number of them referred to the importance of the advice and counsel they received from Peter Drucker. Frustrated, he came home for Christmas vacation hoping to seek Drucker's advice on his planned career. I resisted, not wanting to bother Peter. My wife and son insisted, so I asked Peter to visit. He stunned me by accepting the invitation. He then spent three hours at lunch with my son and me, giving my son career advice. My son left that meeting saying, "I learned as much in those three hours than in three semesters of MBA studies." People were important to Peter.

On our way back to the Drucker home, I asked him when he was going to revise *Management: Tasks, Responsibilities, Practices* so that we could continue to use the book in Claremont. "I am not," he yelled out. Stunned, I said, "Well then how are we going to teach your material?" "Look around," he said, "all the material you need is there."

Then in June 2005, when we were finishing *The Effective Executive in Action*, he said, "I understand you want to revise *The Practice of Management*." I replied, "Oh, no, I want to revise *Management: Tasks, Responsibilities, Practices*." He said, "That is going to be a lot of work." I agreed, and then he said, "Okay." Wow, a

dream come true. Then, with his death on November 11, 2005, came the awareness that I would no longer be able to work with him. It made me sad. While updating and revising that book, I have always tried to ask myself, "What would Peter do?" and then remind myself, "When in doubt, don't," and by all means, "Do not knowingly do harm."

Peter Drucker gave me his time, his help, and opportunities to stretch and to try to do what he couldn't do at that late stage of his life. What a gift he gave me and what wonderful lessons he taught me about the importance of *people* and *integrity in personal relationships*.

Joseph A. Maciariello is the Horton Professor of Management at the Drucker School of Management and director of research at The Drucker Institute. He coauthored "The Daily Drucker" and "The Effective Executive in Action" with Peter F. Drucker, and recently carried on Drucker's legacy by revising two existing Drucker books, "Management: Tasks, Responsibilities, Practices" and "Management Cases."

EGO, CUSTOMER, AND INNOVATION

by Geoff Smart

My face had just turned beet red.

It was five minutes before my university management class was to start and the professor was handing back the papers we had submitted on our career goals. I had written about creating a niche in professional services, to apply expertise in human behavior to help CEOs and investors build valuable companies.

If McKinsey helps its clients solve problems of "what" (products, pricing, and so on), my firm would solve the most important problems of "who" (CEO succession, leadership consulting, and M&A integration). Fixing people problems in companies would mean creating billions in shareholder value.

Apparently, the professor had found my goals a bit lofty. From the front of the room, the bespectacled gentleman motioned for me to approach him. I stood up and with not a little trepidation, made my way to where he was seated. There before me was the already legendary Peter Drucker.

Peter was about to impart a valuable life lesson to me. It was a lesson that would also be imparted to the rest of the class because, as it turned out, his lapel microphone was switched on. His Austrian-accented baritone voice boomed across the amphitheater as he spoke these words in my ear, "Can I tell you something? Nobody likes a young know-it-all!"

After class, I drove Peter home (no, he did not have a chauffeur). He elaborated on his earlier advice: "Along the career path you identified, you will frequently find yourself in a position of having to win the respect and trust of clients and colleagues much older than you. It is important that you hold yourself with a posture of being there *to serve them,* rather than vice versa. You must keep your ego in check."

His lesson in ego management was invaluable. As CEO of ghSMART, the firm that created the niche market I had described in my university class, I have the pleasure today of humbly serving a team of 30 talented colleagues and more than 100 prestigious clients—CEOs of Fortune 500 companies, all 10 of the 10 biggest private equity firms, and over a dozen billionaire entrepreneurs. This level of success would not have been possible if

I had not received the ego-bruising advice from Peter 14 years ago.

Customer: The Most Important Word in Business

From Peter, I learned that the most important word in business is *customer.*

- "The purpose of business is to create and keep a customer."

- "Who is the customer?"

- "What does the customer consider value?"

At ghSMART, we adopted a "customer above all else" approach to business from Day One. We hire people based on a candidate's ability to highly satisfy our CEO and investor clientele. We guarantee client satisfaction. We measure the satisfaction of each client every six months, tie it back to the individual consultant's performance, and publish the rankings across the firm. If you ask any of my colleagues to describe our firm's main value, they would all say, "high client satisfaction."

Our clients value three things: accuracy of recommendation, data and insight, and responsiveness. We have structured all our business processes to maximize our performance in those three areas.

An intense focus on who the customer is, an awareness of the things the customer values, and an unrelenting attention to delivering high customer satisfaction have all been important ingredients in our firm's success.

Innovation: Writing the Rules as You Go

When my colleagues and I founded ghSMART in 1995, we set out on a bold mission to build the "McKinsey of management assessment." The problem was that we did not know anything. We did not know anybody. And we did not have any money.

But, thanks to Peter Drucker, we did have a framework for managing innovation and steering entrepreneurship. Some of his most helpful lessons on innovation:

"Nobody likes a young know-it-all!"

- "The best way to predict the future is to create it."

- "Listen to the whispers of unexpected successes."

- "The three phases of any successful entrepreneurial venture are: 1) realizing that the market is not exactly where you think it is, and being willing to shift focus, 2) becoming suddenly cash-strapped, and 3) outgrowing the capabilities of the founder."

The first two bullet points define the innovative aspect of our culture. Because we are creating the future and listening to the whispers of unexpected successes, it is important that we value communication and experimentation. My experience has not been perfect as CEO in this regard. One mistake I've made is that I have not been as forgiving of mistakes as I should, which leads to hesitation by the team to try new things. However, overall, we have succeeded in being very open and good in communicating what is working and what is not, and continuously improving and solidifying principles that work while shedding those that don't. We take time away from the daily grind to share our lessons—three summits per year, monthly town hall meeting conference calls, and specific service-innovation teams called "interest groups" that allow us to push the boundary on innovation.

That last bullet point was especially helpful. Here is how we applied this advice to the three phases of an entrepreneurial venture that I mentioned earlier.

The market is not exactly where you think it is, so you have to be prepared to shift focus. Early-stage, small companies were our initial target clients. They were excited to buy our services to help them make better bets on the people in whom they would invest and hire. However, we realized that these types of customers were often financially unstable, difficult to satisfy, and extremely price sensitive (unwilling to spend the large fees consulting firms charged). In contrast, we had some experience serving bigger clients, which proved to be more enjoyable and profitable. For example, we served a deadbeat engineering firm as well as a billionaire CEO of a Fortune 500 firm—both in the same month about two years after our founding. You can guess which one turned out to be the better type of client! We therefore shifted to marketing our services to large private equity firms, big corporations, and billionaire deal makers. We discovered that it was much more fun—and much more profitable—to focus on being the trusted adviser to the big kahunas of industry.

Becoming cash-strapped was common for companies during the Great Recession of 2009. Once we recognized that there was trouble ahead, we trimmed some excess costs and held cash rather than pay it out to our employee-shareholders. So far, we've sailed through the recession with no missed payrolls, no cuts in 401(k) matches or health benefits, and no reductions in headcount. In fact, we actually increased our consultant headcount by 14 percent this year.

At ghSMART, it was evident right from the beginning that the firm was outgrowing the founder's capabilities. In 1995, I was a 23-year-old founder and first-time CEO who had not yet developed many skills. I immediately began to surround myself with people who were great at things I was not. This came directly from Peter's advice to "figure out what you are good at, and hire people who can do the rest," which is also found in his classic book, *Innovation and Entrepreneurship.*

Ron Zoibi was hired as our CFO, and he has been a dream come true in managing the Finance and IT sides of the house. We hired seasoned psychologists, superstars from McKinsey, Bain, and BCG, and an extraordinary team of executive assistants.

With the words of Peter Drucker echoing in my head, we set mutually agreed-upon goals and aligned financial incentives. I made sure to get out of my colleagues'

way rather than micromanage their every decision. This approach has allowed us to scale our business smoothly and avoid the bottlenecking trap into which micromanaging founders commonly fall.

The best part of Peter's advice is that it works. As an innovator, we reached a milestone when a Harvard Business School case study was published in 2008, "ghSMART & Co.: Pioneering in Professional Services." The case describes how we applied some of Peter Drucker's advice to define and grow our niche in professional services. Unfortunately, Peter had passed away three years before the case was published. We could not thank him for his advice.

Peter Drucker gave me his excellent advice 14 years ago. I will be forever grateful to him and for his lessons about ego management, the importance of the customer, and innovation.

Geoff Smart is chairman and CEO of ghSMART, a management assessment firm for CEOs and investors, which he founded in 1995. He is co-creator of the Topgrading® approach to talent management, and is co-author of the New York Times best seller "Who: The A Method for Hiring" (Ballantine Books/Random House, 2008). For more information, please see www.ghsmart.com.

HOW PETER DRUCKER INFLUENCED MY PERSONAL AND PROFESSIONAL DEVELOPMENT

by Christian Horak

U p to June 7, 1992, Peter F. Drucker had played only a comparatively small role in my professional and private life. At that time, I was working on my doctoral dissertation (titled "Controlling in NPOs") at the Department of Management at the Vienna University of Economics and Business. While researching the literature, I naturally came across Peter's book *Managing the Nonprofit Organization.* Back then a quick browse was all the book got.

As an assistant professor for management at the Vienna University of Economics and Business, I had come across Peter's work on a regular basis. Back then, I certainly saw him as an important author with great influence on the development of modern business theory, but I ranked many other thinkers and authors on the same level.

In connection with my Ph.D. thesis, I had applied to participate in Session 298 of the Salzburg Seminar in Salzburg, Austria, and was the only German participant to be invited. Peter was part of the faculty of this session and personally attended on the first two days. I hoped to receive significant inputs for my dissertation and thus went to Salzburg with great expectations.

The schedule for Session 298 in the morning of Monday, June 8, 1992, simply said "NPOs & a World in Transition + Discussion (Drucker)."

In general, the first impression one gets of a person is the strongest. In this particular case, that was certainly true. On that morning, I observed a man well advanced in years but

Good intentions are not enough.

extremely youthful both physically and intellectually. It was Peter, and he just sat down on top of his desk, and, dangling his legs, began to explain his point of view in a simple, concise way. His statements were clear and to the point, but first and foremost uncompromising at their core. I tried to take as many notes as possible while at the same time listening carefully. My notes from back then, which I dug out once more for writing this article, include the following:

- Managing NPOs is in general more complex than managing comparable for-profit companies.

- The social sector's task is to have an impact on people and thus change their lives. (NPOs as change agents.)

- Good intentions are not enough.

Starting from these basic statements, the session then went into more detail. I was privileged to be able to further reflect on Peter's thoughts on the topic of "To manage for the mission" in a working group, together with a close companion of Peter's, Frances Hesselbein.

During the 1990s I met Peter time and again at various conferences of what was then the Peter Drucker Foundation (now the Leader to Leader Institute). Whenever we met, it was a formative experience for me. As we were both born in Vienna, it has always been fascinating for me, apart from professional discussions, to talk about his personal history, particularly his time in Vienna as a youth and then at other European locations.

I am still in close contact with Frances Hesselbein, who has been a keynote speaker at the Austrian NPO Congress in Vienna several times. Peter more than once described her as the personality, the leader, who implemented his thoughts on good NPO management most effectively. This is underpinned by the statement, "Girl Scouts of the U.S.A. is one of the best managed organizations I know." For me, Frances is the personified application of Peter's management principles in practice.

Peter Drucker's Influence on My Professional Development

As I look back on my career, I see that Peter has had a major influence on my professional development.

After finishing my doctoral dissertation in 1993, I became a management consultant, and ever since I have been working with NPOs and public administration institutions. In this position I use many of Peter's thoughts and approaches. One of the statements Peter made at the Salzburg Seminar remains crucial for me. It has also become the guiding principle of my work: "Managing NPOs is more complex than managing comparable companies."

I also feel a personal obligation to promote and explain this principle, thus strengthening NPO managers' self-esteem, which traditionally has not been very pronounced in Europe. This task I would call my personal professional mission.

Does, at first glance, this personal professional mission strike you as odd?

Maybe some questions can help underline why this task is also my mission:

- What for-profit company has to move within a pronounced multidimensional system of objectives, where conflicts of objectives are bound to occur and success cannot be measured by purely quantitative indicators?

- What for-profit company has to coordinate the work of extremely different basic types of employees in its personnel management as efficiently as possible (paid and voluntary workers)?

- What for-profit company does not know what prices can be charged several months after the fact for services already rendered?

Generally, the answer to all these questions is "None." For nonprofits, these questions amount to major management challenges.

The five core questions of the self-assessment tool of the Leader to Leader Institute are all relevant in the context of my own development. At first glance, these questions look straightforward, but it is often fiendishly difficult to answer them in practice:

- What is our business (mission)?

- Who is our customer?

- What does the customer consider value?

- What have been our results?

- What is our plan?

The reason it is so difficult to answer these questions is that to answer properly, the NPOs must:

- Remain focused on the real core of their work. (Why are we here? When are we most effective?)

- Remain focused on the actual target group for the services provided. (With whom do we actually want to achieve something? What do we intend to change with these persons?)

- Actively deal with the needs of this most important target group.

- Work on the basis of objectives and be both willing and able to measure whether these objectives have been achieved.

- Be willing to part with things, to enable new developments, and so accomplish the mission more effectively.

If, in my work with NPOs, I succeed in answering these basic questions honestly and uncompromisingly, I achieve the greatest effect for the NPOs. For doing so it is necessary to get to the root, the core of the matter, and not to give up before the real answers to the questions are found. Then the answers often result in substantial actions. Again, the changes at Girl Scouts of the U.S.A. under the leadership of Frances Hesselbein in the 1970s and 1980s can be seen as a prime example.

Therefore, I see it as my task to actively accompany and support NPOs on this path of change, which in general is a hard and challenging one. In doing so, I find Peter's basic questions and the underlying tools (such as the self-assessment tool) extremely useful in providing directions.

In addition to my role as a consultant, my position as a partner and managing director of a large Austrian management consulting agency, Contrast Management Consulting, requires that I answer these basic questions as well as I can and that I have them guide my actions. In this connection, I am responsible for personnel management and coordinating the general process of creating vision and strategy at Contrast. In this role, too, Peter's ideas and guidelines have provided me with support, motivation, and inspiration.

As a knowledge organization, Contrast regards innovation as an absolutely central item. Especially in times of crisis it is thus important for me as a manager to exert healthy optimism and to see "tomorrow as an opportunity." I am trying to follow Drucker's concept that managers do not solve problems but identify and utilize opportunities, and pass this concept on to their employees.

As I am not a natural-born optimist, Peter's guidelines have been immensely helpful. They always lead me back to these questions. Ultimately, we have to create positive energy ourselves and enable positive energy to flow through our whole area of responsibility, as well as the whole enterprise. For this optimistic position I have also profited enormously from Frances Hesselbein, who regards optimism as one of her main attributes and an important part of her success in leadership, and when pursuing a mission.

As a person responsible for managing employees, I am constantly trying to answer these questions that Peter posed:

- Are the best and most successful employees actually used for the most innovative opportunities?

- Are these employees able to look for opportunities systematically?

- Does this search for opportunities take place within a framework of clearly defined processes and is it therefore institutionalized?

Peter Drucker's Influence on My Personal Development

In addition to the concept of optimism, Peter's ideas have certainly influenced me beyond my professional life. His thoughts and his ideas kept me personally focused on things that are really important for me—for example, to be a good father and to stay in good physical shape. Ultimately, the five management questions and the consistent pursuit of objectives can be transferred to personal and private life. In the last few years I benefited greatly from this. I hope to be able to pass on this knowledge to my children.

Conclusion

Writing this article has provided me with the opportunity to address the influence, in the most positive sense imaginable, that Peter Drucker had on me. Altogether, this influence has been extensive. Finally, it is impossible for me to say how my career would have developed if I had not met this great thinker on that day in June 1992, at Leopoldskron Castle in Salzburg.

For this opportunity and the many other wonderful things that I hinted at in this article, I want to express my sincere gratitude to Peter Drucker.

Christian Horak is a partner and head of the Department of Nonprofit and Public Management at Contrast Management Consulting. He is a lecturer at the Institute for Strategic Management and Management Control, and at two MBA programs (social management and health care), at the Vienna University of Economics and Business.

ABOUT THE LEADER TO LEADER INSTITUTE

Established in 1990 as the Peter F. Drucker Foundation for Nonprofit Management, the Leader to Leader Institute furthers its mission—to strengthen the leadership of the social sector—by providing social sector leaders with the essential leadership wisdom, inspiration, and resources to lead for innovation and to build vibrant social sector organizations. It is this essential social sector, in collaboration with its partners in the private and public sectors, that changes lives and builds a society of healthy children, strong families, decent housing, good schools, and work that dignifies, all embraced by the diverse, inclusive, cohesive community that cares about all of its people.

The Leader to Leader Institute provides innovative and relevant resources, products, and experiences that enable leaders of the future to address emerging opportunities and challenges. With the goal of leading social sector organizations toward excellence in performance, the Institute has brought together more than 400 thought leaders to publish over twenty books available in twenty-eight languages and the award-winning quarterly journal *Leader to Leader*.

The Leader to Leader Institute engages social sector leaders in partnerships across the sectors that provide new and significant opportunities for learning and growth. We coordinate unique, high-level summits for leaders from all three sectors and collaborate with local sponsors on workshops and conferences for social sector leaders on strategic planning, leadership, and cross-sector partnerships.

Building on our legacy of innovation, the Leader to Leader Institute explores new approaches to strengthen the leadership of the social sector. With sources of talent and inspiration that range from the local community development corporation to the U.S. Army to the corporate boardroom, we help social sector organizations identify new leaders and new ways of operating that embrace change and abandon the practices of yesterday that no longer achieve results today.

Get to Know the Leader to Leader Institute

See www.leadertoleader.org for information on our programs, resources, and articles from *Leader to Leader*.
Become a member and support our work.

"Don't tell me you had a wonderful meeting with me."

"Tell me what you're going to do on Monday that's different."

This is the challenge that Peter Drucker liked to present to his consulting clients — and it may well be more important now than ever. Indeed, in today's high-stakes environment, it is crucial for you to quickly turn great ideas into real results.

Drucker Unpacked, a new management training tool from the Drucker Institute at Claremont Graduate University, is designed to help you and your colleagues soak in decades of wisdom from the most trusted name in the field and immediately convert these principles into practice.

Please visit our website **(www.DruckerUnpacked.com)** or call our offices today **(Ryan Forsthoff at 770-355-1344)** to learn more about this cost-effective, self-facilitated training system and to find out how to bring Drucker Unpacked's "Business in Action" kits or our full "Drucker Management Path" curriculum to your team!

The Drucker Institute
CLAREMONT GRADUATE UNIVERSITY